Kingfisher

Animal
Series editor: Jonathan Burt

Kingfisher

Ildiko Szabo

REAKTION BOOKS

To Lara, my amazing daughter, who finds wonder everywhere.

Published by
REAKTION BOOKS LTD
Unit 32, Waterside
44–48 Wharf Road
London N1 7UX, UK
www.reaktionbooks.co.uk

First published 2019

Printed and bound in China

A catalogue record for this book is available from the British Library

ISBN 978 1 78914 139 9

Contents

Introduction:
A Realm of Kingfishers

Watching a common kingfisher dive is to witness a moment of perfection. The bird effortlessly cleaves through the water and, in a flash, re-emerges shedding water droplets. From Britain to Japan, the common kingfisher species reigns supreme. It is the most cosmopolitan and northern-dwelling of this predominately tropical family of birds.

The naming of kingfishers is based on European experience. The English appellation of kingfisher, a contraction of 'king's fisher', dates back to at least the 1500s. A more recent explanation of this regal name is that 'king' alludes to a common kingfisher's blue cloak. King George III (1730–1820) challenged clothiers across England to deliver a triumphant colour suitable for utilization by royalty. The sumptuous shade of blue created by Scutts Bridge Factory in Rode, Somerset, won the competition, acquiring the accolade of 'Royal Blue'. Why British kingfishers are called 'fisher' is obvious: it refers to the eye-catching skill, grace and finesse displayed to perfection by these flashy feathered statesmen.

Carl Linnaeus, the Swedish taxonomist who pioneered the genus–species binomial concept, was striving to create a universal biological naming system. Linnaeus knew these birds were called kingfishers in Swedish and possibly that their English name had the same meaning. He was probably equally aware

James Leyland has captured the very moment when this common kingfisher (*Alcedo atthis*) begins to enter the water.

7

Patience, alongside knowing the habits of your local kingfisher, can result in astonishing images, such as this one captured by Andy Morffew of a common kingfisher (*Alcedo atthis*) exiting the water.

that 'icebird' was the translation of their German, Dutch, Danish and Norwegian common name. But he elected to ignore these colloquial names.

What Linnaeus was striving for was a name that needed no explaining, a name already ingrained in the scientific language of his era. He turned to Ovid's 'Myth of the Halcyon' when he named the kingfisher family Alcedinidae and the common kingfisher *Alcedo atthis*.[1] Since the first century, reading extracts of Ovid's *Metamorphoses* in Latin had been part of a classical education. Linnaeus and the majority of the early European taxonomists

Patience, alongside knowing the habits of your local kingfisher, can result in astonishing images, such as this one captured by Andy Morffew of a common kingfisher (*Alcedo atthis*) exiting the water.

The Order of the Garter is on a riband of royal blue. The 'king' in 'kingfisher' is thought to be derived from the birds being robed in royal blue.

would likewise have read *Metamorphoses* in the original, thus gaining a grounding in Roman and Greek mythology. Translations of Ovid's magnum opus abound, including several in English. Shakespeare owned a copy of the Arthur Golding 1567 translation. Scholars have calculated that about 90 per cent of Shakespeare's allusions to classical mythology refer to stories included in this monumental collection of poems.[2] Given the popularity of Ovid's *Metamorphoses*, its use by Shakespeare and other literary and visual artists for literary allusions, and its availability in multiple languages, it is not surprising that early avian taxonomists utilized Ovid when crafting genus and species names. His epitome was a syllabus of characters, a vernacular language uniting European taxonomists.

Following Linnaeus' lead, taxonomists from multiple countries continued to evoke Ovid's epic poem when assigning genera

'Icebird' is the colloquial name for *Alcedo atthis* in German, Dutch, Danish and Norwegian. In winter, these and the crested kingfishers (*Megaceryle lugubris*) of Hokkaido dive through thin ice to capture prey.

names to the kingfisher family. *Ceyx, Clytoceyx, Ceryle, Chloroceryle* and *Megaceryle* are all derived from Ceyx, the male protagonist in the 'Myth of the Halcyon'. *Halcyon, Alcedo* and *Lacedo* are variations of Alcyone, the tragic heroine's name. Rendered down to its simplest elements, this myth is a story of marital fidelity. Upon seeing the drowned body of her husband Ceyx, Alcyone leaps off a cliff into the sea to join her beloved in death. At that instant, the gods transform the couple into kingfishers. Depending on the raconteur, the twists and turns in what motivates the gods to intervene differs, sometimes radically, as does the everlasting happiness of the ill-fated lovers.

Drastically different is the portrayal of the landlubber kingfishers of Down Under. Laughing kookaburras have acquired the persona of jocular pranksters, much famed for their ability to subdue poisonous snakes. Bordering on fiendish, their boisterous chorus conjures up images more akin to hooligans than to the virtuous duo depicted in the 'Myth of the Halcyon'.

The present volume deals extensively with the iconology of the chaste European common kingfisher and their North American counterpart, the belted kingfisher, plus their antithesis, the Australian swashbuckling, laughing kookaburra. The bulk of the kingfisher's appearance in Anglophone culture focuses on these three birds. It is extremely unfair to judge an entire bird family of 114-plus species on only a few iconic ones. Doubly so when considering how diverse, how bizarre and how resourceful the rest of the kingfisher clan is. Many of these lesser-known kingfishers are sensationally beautiful and fascinating in their own right. It is the iridescent plumage of the majority of them that

Herbert Draper's 1915 painting of Halcyone (Alcyone) foreshadows her transformation into a kingfisher; her half-discarded clothing resembles wings. Above her are a pair of kingfishers.

transforms them into dazzling feathered jewels. For the birds themselves, their splendid attire is both a benefit and a curse. Some civilizations have venerated kingfishers, but more commonly they were, and still are in a few regions, hunted for food or for the economic value of their dazzling plumage.

This book explores kingfisher representations in myths, legends, literature, music and popular culture. Before we navigate through this kaleidoscope of birds, it is important to understand their origins, their basic biology and why kingfishers are divided into three distinctive lineages. The triad of Water, Tree and River Kingfishers are all part of the glorious 'realm of kingfishers'.[3]

But first, what is a kingfisher?

At first glance, this kingfisher museum specimen could be mistaken for a South American *Morpho* butterfly. The blue flight feathers of grey-headed kingfishers (*Halcyon leucocephala*) are a most regal, triumphant royal blue.

AMERICAN ORNITHOLOGY

FOR THE HOME AND SCHOOL

PUBLISHED MONTHLY
CHAS. K. REED — WORCESTER, MASS.

1 Fossil Brethren and Living Kin

Kingfishers are supreme carnivores. They deserve equal billing with their cousins, the diurnal and nocturnal raptors (eagles and owls). The Latin word *rapere* (to seize or take by force) is the moniker for the 'raptor' clade of avian killers whose needle-sharp, clawed feet are ideally suited for their method of grasping and killing. Raptors use their feet to squeeze the life out of their prey. With their mighty grip, hawks and eagles are capable of flying while carrying prey nearly half their body weight. Some owls can transport prey two to three times their own weight.[1] Compared with raptors, kingfishers' feet are useless. Their diminutive digits can neither kill nor carry. However, raptors and kingfishers utilize many of the same hunting strategies. Both have extraordinary vision systems due to similar morphological adaptations. Despite their foot handicap, kingfishers are fierce feathered carnivores who scan the ground or water's surface, eagle-eyed and waiting for their next meal to appear as if by magic beneath them.

For over two and a half centuries, people have debated where kingfishers fit into the avian tree of life. Carl Linnaeus' tenth edition of *Systema Naturae* is the starting point of modern avian taxonomy. Published in 1758, Linnaeus named and described all 565 birds known to him. This seminal work includes five kingfishers, all placed in the author's newly minted genus *Alcedo*. In this first attempt to create an avian classification system, Linnaeus

The title of this 1736 etching by Charles Knapton (after Giovanni da Udine) is *A Kingfisher Holding a Fish Skeleton in One Foot*. The fish skeleton is more easily identified than the corvid/generic bird depicted.

established six major bird lineages or orders. He placed kingfishers in the Picae, the woodpecker clan of forest birds. Compared with the dry style of writing in the twenty-first century, William Turton's 1808 translation of Linnaeus' Latin text defining Picae attributes is almost playful:

One of William Morris's designers, William Frend De Morgan, created this red lustreware tile known as *Kingfisher with Beak through Fish.*

Bill sharp-edged, convex above; legs short, strong, feet formed for walking, perching or climbing; body toughish, impure; food various filthy substances; nest in trees; the male feeds the female while she is sitting. They live in pairs.[2]

This suite of characteristics justified lumping kingfishers together with parrots, toucans, hornbills, anis, crows and ravens, rollers, orioles, mynas, birds of paradise, cuckoos, wrynecks, woodpeckers, nuthatches, bee-eaters, hoopoes, tree creepers and hummingbirds. Most of the Latin family names Linnaeus created for these birds are still in use; not surprisingly, how they are grouped (avian phylogeny) is radically different from what he initially proposed.

Hans Gadow's 1893 classification of birds outlined thirteen orders. His order of Coraciiformes places kingfishers with owls, nightjars, rollers, swifts, mousebirds and trogons.[3] With the advent of DNA sequencing, the number of bird orders has grown

Linnaeus economized on printing costs by maximizing the utility of this late 1700s colour plate. He commissioned George Edwards to combine a North American belted kingfisher (*Megaceryle alcyon*) with an Ethiopian succulent plant.

to 41. During the seemingly endless reorganization of the avian family tree, kingfishers have never budged, steadfastly remaining Coraciiformes. The order's namesake, the common raven (*Corvus corax*) has been booted out. Now *C. corax*, along with crows, jays and indeed all the corvids, are nested within Passeriformes, the perching birds (sparrows, robins and so on). Calling kingfishers Coraciiformes still has a grain of truth to it. The root words *corax* and *coracis* have several non-avian meanings that are quite apt for kingfishers. 'Battering ram' or 'hooked war engine' are great descriptors of the mighty beaks sported by most members of the kingfisher clan.

Today's much-reduced Coraciiformes include kingfishers plus rollers, todies, motmots and bee-eaters, all of which are phenomenal birds with sensational plumage. Some are dazzlingly bright, others are more muted, and some have extremely daring and unexpected colour combinations. Ignoring eccentric species, this is a clan of non-migratory perch and aerial hunters of the tropical and temperate zones. In contrast to the majority of birds, most Coraciiformes possess relatively short lower-leg bones and share a particular configuration of leg muscles and tendons; all have partially fused toes. Along with the Bucerotiformes (hornbills, hoopoes and wood hoopoes), they share the same arrangement of palate bones in the roof of their mouths and have a staple middle ear bone (columella) of a particular shape. Taking the Coraciiformes' basic body plan of large head, strong beak, stout body and short, rounded wings, you might say that most kingfishers look top-heavy with their teddy-bear heads and Pinocchio-esque, extra-long, tapered beaks. As a rule of thumb, Coraciiformes beaks are equal to, or twice as long as, the diameter of their heads.

In a 2014 special issue of *Science*, Dr Erich Jarvis and his colleagues presented a new avian family tree using whole-genome studies, placing Coraciiformes into Afroaves. Current thinking is that the Afroaves are all descendants of the same raptor-like theropod ancestor. Eagles, hawks and vultures (Accipitriformes) and owls (Strigiformes) are also members of the Afroaves. In this larger grouping, diurnal and nocturnal raptors, kingfishers and the other Coraciiformes find themselves once again in the company of hornbills, trogons, mousebirds, cuckoo rollers and woodpeckers.[4]

As with their carnivorous relatives in Afroaves, the eagles, hawks and owls, kingfishers have two foveae in each eye. Like humans, the majority of non-predatory birds have only one of these retinal depressions or pits of highly concentrated photo-receptors per eye. Foveae are the site of the eye's finest vision, used by us for reading and other close work. The brain receives information and interprets the images from both eyes; three-dimensional vision occurs where these images overlap. Having double the number of foveae embedded in the typically thicker avian retina accounts for the greater visual acuity these predators possess.

Water Kingfishers have an eye like no other. The green-and-rufous kingfisher (*Chloroceryle inda*), an Amazonian kingfisher, has been extensively researched. Various structures within the eye are unique, as is the location of the temporal fovea. Typically, in eagles and kites, the vision range of the temporal fovea is 15 degrees. In green-and-rufous kingfishers, this same structure has a vision range of 52 degrees. The retinal eye structures that perceive colour are much more complex in birds than in any other class of vertebrates. Oil droplets, thought to be inherited from theropod dinosaur ancestors, are present in coelacanths, lungfish, diurnal reptiles, turtles, birds, monotremes and marsupials.[5] Human eyes and those of all placental mammals, amphibians, snakes and crocodiles do not have oil droplets. The current theory is that oil

Green-and-rufous kingfishers (*Chloroceryle inda*) are denizens of tropical American freshwater wetlands, forest streams and intertidal mangrove swamps.

droplets enhance colour vision by increasing discrimination and the number of hues in an animal's 'colour space'. Green-and-rufous kingfishers, and a few other avian species that dive through water to capture prey, have a preponderance of red oil droplets in their retinae. These droplets may reduce glare or help neutralize the dispersion of light from particulate matter in water.[6] Studies of laughing kookaburras found five different types of oil droplets in each of the four types of single-cones-plus-oil-droplets in one type of double cone. Like quails and other ground-feeding birds, kookaburras have an overabundance of red oil droplets, which is thought to help discriminate darker colours such as brown in monochromatic substrates.[7] This facilitates the finding of seeds (quails) or arthropods (kingfishers).

A significant amount of visual processing goes on at the retinal level in birds. In effect, the avian retina 'digitizes' an image and sends a far more processed version to the avian brain than the human retina sends to ours. Other than having four images to process, another potential neurological-processing nightmare happens when both the predator and prey are moving. When hovering, kingfishers, hawks and other avian predators keep their heads rock-steady relative to the ceaseless movements of their wings and body. This hovering frenzy, this aerial dance whose objective is the acquisition of steady images, is necessary to accurately calculate prey position.

For aerial aquatic predators, add the additional problem of distortion inherent in the air/water interface, which alters the

This pied kingfisher (*Ceryle rudis*) composite by Charles J. Sharp shows how the body shape of the bird changes from flight to dive mode.

apparent position of prey. Prey depth determines dive angle, with deeper prey requiring steeper dive angles. Steep dive angles have two advantages: they increase decent speed, and they reduce water-refraction effects regarding the apparent, versus the actual, location of prey. Once submerged, kingfisher eyes must instantly adjust to the challenges of functioning in water, a medium much denser than air. The asymmetrical lens of aquatic kingfishers suggests that image-focusing switches from the nasal fovea to the temporal fovea when the bird is underwater. The brain-processing abilities of kingfishers are not trivial.

Though distinctive, kingfisher eye morphology is not of much help when trying to identify an avian fossil taxon from a smashed heap of bones. It is more useful to look for variations of the unusual arrangement of palate bones and staple middle-ear columella bone, which kingfishers share with other Coraciiformes and Bucerotiformes. Finding a relatively short tarsometatarsus – the bone that connects the ankle to the toes – is helpful. Knowing that, zeroing in on the toe bones is key.

Iconically, non-aquatic birds' feet are drawn as matchstick-type affairs with three toes facing forwards and one facing backwards. Technically that formula applies to kingfishers. They have a hind toe, which in many bird orders is rudimentary or missing. The broad base of their two or three forward-facing toes is fused for much of their length, resulting in a foot with a sole. So reminiscent is this of a mammalian foot that, out of context, the imprint or a drawing of such a footprint could be mistaken for some sort of tree-climbing animal or extra-terrestrial creature. What separates kingfishers from the rest of the syndactyl (fused-toe) foot clan is an extremely small detail. Instead of having the second toe (outer) fused to the third (middle) for the most of its length, the third toe is inseparably fused to the fourth (inner). Or, more simply put, when kingfishers have both feet together, they have the equivalent of a free-standing diminutive index finger. In hornbills, rollers and bee-eaters, the free digit is on the outside of the foot like an outstretched pinkie.

Compared with some of their colossal dinosaur progenitors, finding isolated fossilized bird bones is near miraculous due to the fragile nature of these often tiny body parts. Compound this with the reality that few land birds die where their remains are instantly buried in sediment. As remains true today, dead birds are preyed upon by carnivorous animals who might consume or disperse the bones. Rodents, ants, maggots and numerous invertebrates all take their toll gnawing on the connective tissue that binds bones together.

Bone fossilization requires a whole suite of circumstances to be 'just right', not only for the initialization of the lengthy mineralization process but also for the bones to remain together and withstand the great pressures involved, and subsequently for geological folding or erosion to enable the bones to be 'found'. Not surprisingly, small birds are poorly represented in fossil deposits, and our knowledge of their evolutionary history is not as complete as it is for large reptiles and mammals. W. Pierce Brodkorb estimated that, between the time of *Archaeopteryx* and the present, up to 1.6 billion species of birds probably have existed, yet we have specimen evidence for less than 1 per cent.[8] Fossils dating from the late Jurassic to the K–Pg extinction (157–65 MYA) contain toothed birds such as *Hesperornis*, *Ichthyornis* and *Archaeopteryx*. From the Eocene (56–35 MYA) onwards, bird fossils become increasingly plentiful, with many forms closely resembling those living today. In fact, it is most probable that all living bird orders arose before or during the Eocene. Kingfishers were part of this Eocene radiation.[9]

Tracing the kingfisher lineage got off to a promising start when in 1846 Sir Richard Owen, biologist, comparative anatomist, paleontologist and founder of the British Natural History Museum, described *Halcyornis toliapicus*, seventeen years before the world's best known avian fossil, *Archaeopteryx* (Meyer, 1861), was discovered. *Halcyornis* is a lower Eocene fossil from the blue London Clay formation.[10] This latter specimen, unearthed in the county of Kent, England, was the first fossil bird ever documented, named and published. Owen could have named it anything he wished. By following Linnaeus' lead and invoking the 'Myth of the Halcyon', he underscored his conviction that *Halcyornis* was a kingfisher. It has since come to light that Owen appropriated the *Halcyornis* discovery. Today, this fossil's official name is '*Halcyornis toliapicus* Koenig, 1825', in recognition of the person who discovered it and the year it was found.

Since 1846, the diversity of bird fossils discovered, and our growing knowledge of birds in general, has resulted in the re-examination and reclassification of many fossil taxa. In the intervening centuries, *Halcyornis* has had a particularly chequered career, having been considered at one time to be a gull, then a parrot and now perhaps to merit its own extinct bird family, potentially related to either rollers (one of the Coraciiformes) or that problematic quintet, the Madagascar cuckoo-rollers, which have no known living relatives.[11] In 2011, a new generation of British palaeontologists using 3D cross-sectional micro-X-ray techniques looked inside fossil *Halcyornis* skulls. Stig Walsh and Angela Milner focused on the inner ear, the olfactory lobes and the parts of the avian brain responsible for processing sensory stimuli. It turns out that *Halcyornis* had a hearing sensitivity within the upper range of living birds, a reasonably good sense of smell (not common in modern birds) and a high degree of visual specialization.[12] This early Eocene bird (living between 56 and 47.8 MYA) had a very sophisticated sensory skill set. Unfortunately, Walsh and Milner concurred that *Halcyornis* is not a kingfisher.

This syndactyl belted kingfisher (*Megaceryle alcyon*) foot has partially fused front toes resulting in a broad-based foot. In keeping with most Coraciiformes, kingfishers have relatively short tarsometatarsus bones in their lower leg.

Currently, the diminutive *Quasisyndactylus longibrachis* is the oldest 'kingfisher' fossil.[13] It is ancestral to four out of six of the order's families, a sub-group referred to as the Alcediniformes: kingfishers, todies, motmots and bee-eaters. This tiny bird was exhumed at the German middle Eocene Messel site (48–38 MYA).[14] Probable kingfisher fossils from the lower Eocene deposits in Wyoming, at middle Eocene sites in Germany and at Eo-Oligocene sites (34–23 MYA) in France are under investigation.[15] On the other side of the globe at the Australian Queensland Riversleigh deposits (Miocene, 23–5 MYA), a much younger fossil is currently the oldest Tree Kingfisher fossil.

Fossils tell many stories and are not always about the quest to know what came first. Not all fossils are of extinct species. Many Quaternary kingfisher fossils (2 MYA and younger) are indistinguishable from living species. Their existence provides equally valuable pieces in the puzzle for determining region of origin and the recreation of dispersal patterns. Finding red-backed kingfisher (*Todiramphus pyrrhopygius*),[16] azure kingfisher (*Alcedo azurea*), laughing kookaburra (*Dacelo novaeguineae*) and sacred kingfisher (*A. sanctus*) fossils in Australia confirms that they have been residents of that continent for a long time. Likewise, the finding of white-throated kingfisher fossils (*Halcyon smyrnensis*) in Israel; common kingfisher fossils (*A. atthis*) in England and other European countries; belted kingfisher fossils (*Megaceryle alcyon*) in several deposits in North America; and Amazon kingfisher fossils (*Chloroceryle amazona*) in Brazil confirms that they are all long-time residents of these regions. Even more exciting is when a species is found where it no longer lives. Today, giant kingfishers (*M. maxima*) are confined to sub-Saharan Africa. The finding of giant kingfisher fossils in Israel indicates that this species once lived in the Middle East and possibly the entire Mediterranean Basin.[17] At the Florida Thomas

Quasisyndactylus longibrachis is the oldest known fossil Coraciiformes. It is ancestral to kingfishers and todies. This tiny bird was unearthed at Messel, a middle Eocene site in Germany.

Farm site, a 2 MYA fossil *Ceryle* was found. The only living relative of this fossil is the pied kingfisher, a bird that today calls Africa and Asia home.[18] The discovery of extinct rhinoceroses at the same Florida site makes the presence of an extinct relative of the African and Asian pied kingfisher not as contradictory as it might seem. The unearthing of future kingfisher fossils will expand our knowledge of how long kingfishers have inhabited different regions, helping to confirm or disprove current theories about where this clan of carnivores originated and why they live where they do today.

Alfred Russel Wallace commented on the global unequal distribution of kingfishers in 1871:

> There is no part of the world so rich in peculiar forms of bird-life as America, more especially the southern half of it, yet it is the poorest of all parts of the world in kingfishers, only eight species being found in the whole continent – a continent with more rivers and more fish than any other! The single island of Celebes [Sulawesi, Indonesia] actually contains as many different kinds of kingfisher as all North and South America, while New Guinea contains more than twice as many . . . It is perhaps even a more extraordinary fact that there is no peculiar type of kingfisher in America, all the eight species belonging to one genus, and that genus found also in Europe, Asia, and Africa . . . Not only has it [the Celebes] eight peculiar species and three peculiar genera, but one of the latter has affinities with an African genus.[19]

In 1992, Hilary and Kathie Fry theorized a Malesia origin for kingfishers based on the high kingfisher specioseness in this region plus the supposition of terrestrial sit-and-wait predators

Johann Baptist Zwecker's *Scene in New Guinea, with Characteristic Animals* was commissioned by Alfred Russel Wallace for his book *The Geographical Distribution of Animals*, vol. 1. The caption identifies the bird as a racket-tailed king-hunter (*Tanysiptera galatea*).

being an ancestral trait.[20] The incredible kingfisher diversity east of Wallace's line in Australasia is likely to be the result of the complex geography of Malesia in the Miocene.[21] Today the region has an overabundance of islands, creating an extremely isolated and complex landscape perfect for biodiversification.

In 2017, Dr Michael Andersen and his colleagues calculated that the common ancestor of all kingfishers evolved approximately 27.1 MYA in the Indomalayan region. The modern subfamilies of Water Kingfishers (Cerylinae) and Tree Kingfishers (Daceloninae – formerly the Halcyoninae) diverged from each other approximately 25 MYA. The River Kingfishers (Alcedininae) are akin to the new kid on the kingfisher block, having diversified much later; the Alcedininae modern genera appeared only 7 MYA.[22]

This interest in unravelling kingfisher systematics is not a recent development. In the 13 April 1871 edition of the then recently founded magazine *Nature*, Alfred Russel Wallace penned a book review for the 'Our Book Shelf' section. The book in question, *A Monograph of the Alcedinidae; or, Family of Kingfishers*, contained according to Wallace 'A copious account of the literature of the family . . . no less than 135 separate works being enumerated, with references to every species of kingfisher described or noticed in them.' It took Richard Bowdler Sharpe, the librarian of the Zoological Society of London, from 1868 until 1871 to compile, commission illustrations for, and write what was then the definitive work on the 125 kingfisher species known to the Western world. Sharpe divided kingfishers into two subfamilies: the Alcedinidae, or 'true kingfishers', characterized by a vertically compressed, keeled beak; and the Daceloninae, or 'king-hunters', which have a horizontally depressed beak, rounded or furrowed above.[23] Unfortunately Sharpe's 'king-hunters' did not take; this wonderfully descriptive appellation is no longer part of the kingfisher lexicon.

This cladogram is a visual representation of the relatedness of kingfisher genera to each other and to other Coraciiformes (birds not to scale). This phylogeny of 21 of the 35 genera of Coraciiformes is based on 3,249 ultraconserved element loci (Andersen Lab, University of New Mexico, 2017).

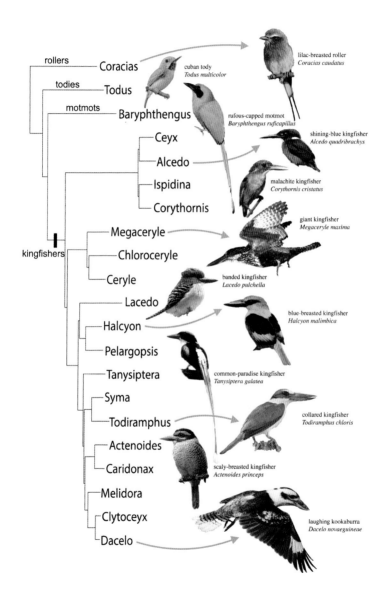

rollers

todies

motmots

kingfishers

Coracias

Todus

Baryphthengus

Ceyx

Alcedo

Ispidina

Corythornis

Megaceryle

Chloroceryle

Ceryle

Lacedo

Halcyon

Pelargopsis

Tanysiptera

Syma

Todiramphus

Actenoides

Caridonax

Melidora

Clytoceyx

Dacelo

lilac-breasted roller
Coracias caudatus

cuban tody
Todus multicolor

rufous-capped motmot
Baryphthengus ruficapillus

shining-blue kingfisher
Alcedo quadribrachys

malachite kingfisher
Corythornis cristatus

giant kingfisher
Megaceryle maxima

banded kingfisher
Lacedo pulchella

blue-breasted kingfisher
Halcyon malimbica

common-paradise kingfisher
Tanysiptera galatea

collared kingfisher
Todiramphus chloris

scaly-breasted kingfisher
Actenoides princeps

laughing kookaburra
Dacelo novaeguineae

Richard B. Sharpe's monograph divided kingfishers into two sub-families: the Alcedinidae, or 'true kingfishers', which have vertically depressed, keeled beaks, as exemplified by this blue-eared kingfisher (*Alcedo meninting*) . . .

. . . and the Daceloninae, or 'king-hunters', which sport a horizontally compressed, rounded (or furrowed) beak as seen in this laughing kookaburra (*Dacelo novaeguineae*).

Today the number of recognized kingfisher species varies from 114 to 120, depending on which taxonomic list you consult. This number is sure to increase as recently proposed new species are verified and incorporated onto the lists. It is going to take a decade or more before systematic research using genetic tools is finished. After this is completed, the avian taxonomic community may, or may not, reach a consensus on exactly how many kingfisher species there are. Appendix 1 to this book lists the 114 accepted kingfisher species as per the International Ornithology Congress (IOC) World Bird List (version 8.1). Numbers in brackets after a genus name indicate the number of species the IOC recognizes for that genus.

In the literature, there is debate on how to refer to the three kingfisher lineages. The unresolved question is: Does each of the

In skeletons, the beak differences of Richard B. Sharpe's two sub-families of 'true kingfishers' and 'king-hunters' is apparent. The common kingfisher (*Alcedo atthis*) has a beak that is thinner and vertically compressed. The beak of the laughing kookaburra (*Dacelo novaeguineae*) is broader, rounded and horizontally compressed.

The blurred finger in this photograph is both a perch and a reference scale demonstrating how truly minute rufous-backed dwarf kingfishers (*Ceyx rufidorsa*) are.

three subfamilies merit being elevated to a family of its own? Members of this triad of kingfishers are morphologically quite distinct one from the other. Regardless of their official standing as subfamilies or families, in the scientific literature and elsewhere they are unequivocally segregated into three groups.

When referring to the colloquial names of these three groups, I have elected to capitalize them to differentiate them from kingfisher common names. To some, this ignoring of classical capitalization conventions will seem presumptuous, but it does help the reader to differentiate and recognize that woodland kingfishers and forest kingfishers are two species of Tree Kingfishers. More correctly, the kingfisher triad are known as the Alcedinae (future Alcedinidae) Water Kingfishers, the Cerylinae (future Cerylidae) River Kingfishers and the Daceloninae (future Dacelonidae) Tree or Wood Kingfishers.

The convention of which group is known as River Kingfishers versus Water Kingfishers has an arbitrary air to it. The words 'river' and 'water' should not be taken too literally. Water Kingfishers do live along rivers and beside oceans, and many are equally happy living along large lakes. The terms 'Old World' and 'New World' could have been chosen instead, as for monkeys and other taxa, but this nomenclature would actually be even worse, leading to even greater confusion.

RIVER KINGFISHERS (*Subfamily Alcedinae*)

River Kingfishers, or the small blue or rufous kingfishers, are the most homogeneous members of the kingfisher triads. They are divided into four genera: *Ispidina* (2), *Corythornis* (4), *Alcedo* (7) and *Ceyx* (21). With a total of 34 species, they account for 30 per cent of the world's kingfisher species. Like peas in a pod, all Alcedinidae River Kingfishers have ultra-compact bodies with only a stub of a tail. None have untidy crests or long tails to break up their plump body contours. Their heads melt into their bodies with only a slight suggestion of a neck. They possess the classic kingfisher exaggerated dagger-shaped beak, which in some species is a dazzling carmine-red.

River Kingfishers are akin to brilliant jewels. If you liken Water Kingfishers to noisy, long-tailed dragonflies announcing their presence, then River Kingfishers would be the avian stand-ins for opalescent jewel beetles humming by. When the sun reflects off River Kingfisher plumage, unaccustomed viewers are mesmerized. Be it the iridescent streak down the back or an iridescent wing patch akin to an inlaid polished gemstone, the imperial splendour of this group of kingfishers rivals Fabergé's creations.

A subset of River Kingfishers are one-third the weight and size of Britain's common kingfisher. These exquisite miniatures are called dwarf kingfishers or pygmy kingfishers. Imagine the weight of a £1 or £2 coin in your hand. Holding an African dwarf kingfisher (*Ispidina picta*) would have the equivalent heft of between 9 and 11 grams (0.31–0.38 oz).

River Kingfishers are mainly distributed in the Afrotropics and the Orient, with only one species in Europe, Linnaeus' *Alcedo atthis*. Originally the genera *Ceyx* and *Alcedo* were defined by plumage colour and lifestyle, with the forest-dwelling *Ceyx* having rufous plumage and the water-centric, fish-eating *Alcedo* having some or copious amounts of blue plumage. The reality is a mishmash. Genetic work revealed that rufous colouring has evolved multiple times.[24] Affinities for water and pescatarian abilities have evolved multiple times too. Even though species within a genus are now sorted genetically rather than by colour and behaviour, River Kingfishers remain the most morphologically uniform of the three kingfisher groups.

WATER KINGFISHERS (*Subfamily Cerylinae*)

With a total of nine species, Water Kingfishers account for 7 per cent of the world's kingfisher species. These Cerylinae kingfishers are divided into three genera – *Megaceryle* (4), *Ceryle* (1) and *Chloroceryle* (4) – and are distinctive in a totally different way. The lack of iridescent plumage is a reliable method to distinguish the nine Water Kingfishers from their cousins, the River Kingfishers. Unfortunately, this cannot be applied universally; a very few dull-plumaged Tree Kingfishers shatter this rule of thumb. If confronted with an unknown non-iridescent kingfisher, observing that it has a shaggy crest in addition to noting that the substantial tail is of the type seen on jays (that is, the tail is nearly as long as the body, plus each of the tail feathers is roughly the same length and width) confirms that it is a Water Kingfisher. The nine Water

This shining-blue kingfisher (*Alcedo quadribrachys*) has the previously compulsory colouration of *Alcedo* species: a blue back, blue cap and rufous belly. River kingfishers, with their stubby tails and compact bodies, can be likened to iridescent jewel beetles.

The lack of blue plumage was formerly used to separate *Ceyx* and *Corythomis* from *Alcedo* River Kingfishers. Genetic analysis has confirmed that this Madagascar pygmy kingfisher (*Corythomis madagascariensis*) is related to congeners with blue plumage.

This John James Audubon painting is in the style of a preliminary drawing complete with notations and detailed sketches of flight feathers (c. 1851 or earlier). The double crest of this belted kingfisher (*Megaceryle alcyon*) is correct and rarely depicted so clearly.

Kingfishers encompass both dwarf and giant species. Roughly equivalent to a rook or an American crow in size, the giant king-fisher lives up to its species epithet of *maxima*. It is the largest of all the kingfishers, wielding a mighty 10-centimetre beak.

Water Kingfishers originated in Asia and colonized the New World twice. The *Chloroceryle* arrived first in the New World approximately 8 MYA.[25] The genus is well named. *Chloro*, 'green' in Greek, refers to their predominately green wings and backs. Their underparts are either rufous or white, often sporting neck-ties or waistcoats in a contrasting colour. At some point in the Pliocene, either in the Americas or after having reinvaded the Old World, a common ancestor of the *Chloroceryle* or one of them evolved into the *Ceryle*. Either way, some birds crossed the Atlantic and reinvaded the Old World. By losing the structural green colouration that overlays the dark plumage on their wings and back, they became the stark black-and-white pied kingfisher (*Ceryle rudis*), the only kingfisher devoid of colour.

The *Megaceryle* are thought to have originated in the same area as the *Chloroceryle* but arrived in the New World much later, approximately 1.9 MYA. Their plumage is very similar to the *Chloroceryle* but with more exaggerated, longer and shaggier double Mohawk/punk-style head crests. All traces of green are gone, having been replaced with dull blue-grey or black plumage. Except for the crested kingfisher (*Megaceryle lugubris*), females have the more colourful and complex plumage pattern of the pair. At some point, the *Megaceryle* kingfisher lineage likewise reinvaded the Old World, evolving into the giant kingfisher, which still lives today in sub-Saharan Africa. Some of these kingfisher colonizers spread eastwards, evolving into the crested kingfisher of Southeast

Giant kingfishers (*Megaceryle maxima*) are one of the New World Water Kingfishers which colonized Africa. This image of an adult female preparing for take-off beautifully captures her deep rufous underwing coverts, breast and belly. Males have white and black barred underwing coverts and belly.

The four *Chloroceryle* kingfishers are truly green. Like wrens, many species of kingfishers cock their tails when preparing to vocalize, as seen in this female Amazon kingfisher (*Chloroceryle amazona*).

Asia. Calling these long-tailed, shaggy-headed kingfishers Water Kingfishers is a constant reminder that they are of New World origin.

TREE (OR WOOD) KINGFISHERS (*Subfamily Daceloninae*)

Daceloninae is the largest, most bizarre and heterogeneous of the three kingfisher groups. It is divided into twelve genera: *Actenoides* (6), *Melidora* (1), *Lacedo* (1), *Tanysiptera* (9), *Cittura* (1), *Clytoceyx* (1), *Dacelo* (4), *Pelargopsis* (3), *Caridonax* (1), *Halcyon* (11), *Syma* (2), plus the most speciose of all kingfisher genera, *Todiramphus* (31). With a total of 71 species, they account for 62 per cent of the world's kingfisher species. Sometimes these dwellers of the Old World tropics are referred to as 'the kookaburras and the halcyons'. None are true underwater divers, and only a few have a propensity for feeding in shallow water to procure crustaceans, aquatic insects or the occasional accidental fish. They are

The well-named pied kingfisher (*Ceryle rudis*) is the only kingfisher species that is entirely black and white. When perched, the crest of a pied kingfisher is always visible.

Any kingfisher sporting a shaggy crest is by default a Water Kingfisher – but not all Water Kingfishers have prominent crests. The long tail and ragged crest of this male belted kingfisher are evident.

The best known of the four kookaburras has the dullest plumage of the lot. This rufous-bellied (*Dacelo gaudichaud*) and the spangled kookaburra (*D. tyro*) (not shown) with its bright blue back and spotted head feathers are much more striking.

the group of kingfishers where the appellation of 'kingfishers' is not only erroneous but laughable. Starke's 'king-hunter' was a far superior and more factually accurate name.

The Tree Kingfishers are not only the most diverse group of the triad; they are the most outlandish and the most eccentric. The *Halcyon* genus has brilliant royal blue to turquoise iridescent feathers. Complex altering patterning within a single feather is rare in kingfishers, but a few Tree Kingfishers have attained this feature. As their name suggests, spotted kingfishers (*Actenoides lindsayi*) are spotted. Equally so is the head of the spangled kooka-burra (*Dacelo tyro*). The plumage differences between the sexes of banded kingfishers (*Lacedo pulchella*) are so distinctive that the female and males were almost described as two different species.

Brown-winged kingfishers (*Pelargopsis amauroptera*) have exceptionally long red beaks. When in flight, or seen from behind, the turquoise-hued iridescent upper tail coverts are in sharp contrast to the rest of its brown-hued plumage.

Their trademark is fine barring of white and brown (females) or predominately white and blue, and some brown (males).

Many of the Tree Kingfishers are flashy, but the tails of the paradise kingfishers (*Tanysiptera* sp.) trump the lot. In birds, the 'paradise' moniker is a heads-up that birds so named sport long, spectacular tails (birds of paradise, paradise flycatchers, paradise kingfishers and so on). Racket-tailed king-hunters, the former name of common paradise kingfishers, refers to the naked central tail-feather shafts of these birds, ending in a spoon-shaped feathered section, referred to as a 'racket'. This feather shape is by no means unusual in the class Aves. In *The Descent of Man* (1871), Charles Darwin remarks: 'It is a curious fact that the feathers of species belonging to very distinct groups have been modified in almost exactly the same peculiar manner.'[26] Darwin then goes on to note that these long, bare feather shafts terminating in an 'outburst of feather vanes' occur in the tails of certain hummingbirds, parrots, drongos, birds of paradise, all motmots and all paradise kingfishers.

The blue-breasted kingfisher (*Halcyon malimbica*) is a stunning bird. In addition to its brilliant plumage, it is one of many kingfishers that have a brightly coloured beak.

Laughing kookaburras (*Dacelo novaeguineae*) are by far the best known of the Dacelonids. I saw my first dozen laughing kookaburras while whizzing along a highway in New South Wales; sitting on various fence posts near playgrounds, houses and other random spots, they completely shattered my naive preconception

that this iconic bird was part of the mystique of the Aussie Outback. Their outrageous laugh, large size, conspicuous use of human structures and occasional theft of human edibles make them a hard bird to ignore.

The likelihood of seeing some of the maddeningly elusive forest-dwelling Tree Kingfishers has resulted in a scarcity of information. The observations that do exist are mostly sound recordings or feeding accounts. Once known as the earthworm-eating kingfisher, the shovel-billed kingfisher (*Clytoceyx rex*) is a

Laughing kookaburras are not the only dull-coloured kingfisher. This scaly-breasted *Actenoides princeps* has sombre plumage.

Tree and Water Kingfishers have a prominent tail and broad wings typical of corvids, thrushes and a myriad of other land birds. This flight shot by Jim Bendon captures the wing and tail shape of a laughing kookaburra (*Dacelo novaeguineae*).

most un-kingfisher-like bird, with its freakish beak halfway between those of a hawfinch and a boat-billed heron. Despite this armature, they can (and do) pull earthworms out of soil much like a robin does. Observations of hook-billed kingfishers (*Melidora macrorrhina*) with mud-caked beaks suggest that they too might be diggers, but this equally elusive species has not been caught in the act – yet.

The extremely numerous *Todiramphus* species and, to a lesser extent, *Actenoides* species are the focus of 'speciation-in-action' research. Similar to the story of the Galápagos finches, island isolation has resulted in kingfishers living on different islands of the same archipelago having distinctive plumage from their kin

The word 'paradise' is used to describe Asian long-tailed birds such as birds of paradise, paradise flycatchers and the equally long-tailed paradise kingfishers. Paradise kingfishers have two central tail feathers ending in bright white rackets (or paddles).

on the island next door.[27] Sometimes they are genetically the same, sometimes not.

Beginning with Linnaeus's ruminations and amplified when the first bird fossil was found, attempts to define and decipher kingfisher lineages and their geographic origins have provoked much thought and multiple theories. All in all, these charismatic members of the Coraciiformes have a rich history in the scientific literature. When identifying kingfishers, it is essential to note the exquisite plumage patterns, but it is more important to concentrate on the overall body shape and tail type. Knowing which kingfisher lineage a particular bird belongs to is very informative. Research by palaeontologists has revealed that kingfishers are

world travellers, having colonized Africa six times and the New World twice.[28] Regardless of whether they are members of the River, Tree or Water triad, all kingfishers are feisty, astute hunters, having probably inherited these traits from their Afroaves ancestor. Kingfishers' bravery and prowess are equal to the skill and determination exemplified by their Afroaves cousins, the eagles and the owls.

Frog is clearly on the menu for this Oriental dwarf kingfisher (*Ceyx erithaca*).

2 Kingfishers Unmasked

Did the fidelity of common kingfishers inspire the 'Myth of the Halcyon', or was the halcyon story looking for a suitable animal into which to be transmuted, metamorphosed? The chaste nature of common kingfishers' mating behaviour, and the fidelity and teamwork of the kingfisher couple, are representative of the majority of the kingfisher clan. Simplicity itself is the courtship, the parental cooperation and the partitioning of labour as regards to nest excavation, incubation and feeding of the chicks of this beloved denizen of English streams and waterways. What might be overlooked both in Ovid's poem and while observing common kingfishers along a riverbank is that they are not gregarious. They do not join multispecies mixed flocks and are especially wary of their own kind. Kingfisher couples relentlessly defend their favourite fishing spots and the area around their burrows. After the breeding season, not much changes if the pair elects to stay on the same territory for the remainder of the year. Thinking of kingfisher couples as antisocial, quarrelsome defenders of their food larder is not at odds with their characterization in the 'Myth of the Halcyon' as avian incarnations of true matrimonial bliss.

In a common kingfisher tableau, it takes a practised eye to discern who is Alcyone and who is Ceyx, since both sexes have identical plumage. Only the bottom section of the beak is different. The lower mandibles of females are predominately orange-pink, ending in a small black tip. In males, the black tip is much more conspicuous, extending nearly half the length of the lower beak. During courtship, the identity of the characters comes to light. Only the male offers food. Ceyx, in his feathered form, presents Alcyone with a fish or other delicacy in a gentlemanly fashion by offering it to her head first. This allows her to elegantly swallow the morsel without having to reposition it. Copulation follows with the male sitting on the female's back. After the knot is tied, a kingfisher couple participate equally in all activities, be it chasing intruders, making territorial calls or taking turns digging the nesting burrows.

Perhaps J.R.R. Tolkien was thinking of the burrow of a common kingfisher when he formulated the first sentence of *The Hobbit*: 'In a hole in the ground there lived a hobbit. Not a nasty, dirty, wet hole, filled with the ends of worms and an oozy smell, nor yet a dry, bare, sandy hole.'[1] This phrasing has a discerning air about it. If we are lucky enough to spy a kingfisher burrow as we stroll along a river, its secluded and tidy appearance evokes an appealing oasis of calm. Kingfishers do exert substantial energy in finding the perfect place – the perfect soil type along a riverbank with clear running water – before beginning to dig their burrows.

Luckily for kingfishers, suitable banks occur naturally in steep terrain and along banks of rivers and lakes, plus man-made banks abound along roads, ditches, gravel pits and mining sites. The norm for River and Water Kingfishers is to excavate a burrow that slopes slightly uphill, ending in a bulbous chamber where the eggs are laid on bare earth. The most typical scenario is for both males and females to fly at speed into the earthen bank of choice, chipping a hole with their beaks supplemented by digging with their clawed feet. This foot action helps to enlarge the burrow and facilitates dirt removal. The burrow having a slight upwards slant deters rain from entering. It is not unusual for trial holes to be dug and abandoned. This is especially true if tree roots, rocks or other obstacles are encountered, or, as happens occasionally, if one of the pair dies due to a skull concussion. These tunnels are between 1 and 2 metres (3–6 ft, approx.) in length depending on the species and hardness of the substrate, the current record holder being a staggering 8.5-metre (27 ft 11 in.) tunnel made by the giant kingfisher.[2] Curiously, or possibly a case of convergent architectural evolution, wolf dens and kingfisher burrows are very similar. Wolves typically dig a 4-metre (13 ft) tunnel also with a slight uphill slope ending in a bulbous chamber just big enough for the she-wolf to turn around in.[3]

Common kingfishers' courtship is short. Rather than expending energy on elaborate courtship rituals, the pair concentrate their efforts on the raising of two to three broods in quick succession. During the day, the couple take turns incubating the eggs or nestlings, but only the female incubates at night. Reports exist of common kingfishers laying eggs in a second nest burrow before the first brood of nestlings has fledged in the original one.[4] Most species rear only one brood per year. If the first clutch is lost to predation or other causes, kingfishers usually start a second replacement clutch. The norm is for kingfishers to lay two or three eggs. Belted and common kingfishers are superb breeders, laying unusually large clutches and hatching six to seven chicks per brood. This fecundity matches the concept of Alcyone as the dutiful wife and reflects on her own family background of being one of seven sisters.

The courtship of woodland kingfishers (*Halcyon senegalensis*) is a choreographed affair. High up in the treetops, a couple faces each other while trilling loudly with their beaks half open and their tails cocked over their backs, wren-fashion. This is interrupted when one or both of the birds rigidly opens its wings. Pivoting on their feet, they rotate their bodies slowly, showing

off their bright white wing patches, the white being intensified by the surrounding dark flight feathers. The couple executes this wing-inspection manoeuvre independently or at the same time for one to two seconds, sometimes for up to seven seconds. The current record is fifteen repetitions.[5] White-throated kingfisher (*Halcyon smymensis*) couples also vocalize and shimmy-dance with outspread wings. Previously unknown for the kingfisher clan, one record exists of a white-throated kingfisher flying 60 metres (197 ft) above the trees, vocalizing and then performing a display flight as it spiralled back down to the trees.[6] This is standard behaviour for skylarks, snipes and several other types of bird but most unusual for a kingfisher.

As they survey their realm, perched common kingfishers (*Alcedo atthis*) often have a tranquil air about them. If the beak is completely black in this species, the bird is a male.

An interactive dance best describes the courtship of paradise kingfishers (*Tanysiptera* sp.). The male chases the female in wide circles around a potential nest site. These chases are interrupted briefly when both birds land on, or near, the site in question and start calling to each other. This New Guinea and Australian kingfisher genus typically excavates nests in termitaria. Using only active termitaria yields many benefits. They are natural

Collecting an entire kingfisher burrow to add to a museum nest collection is a challenge. Instead, Dr William W. Ralph collected this soil in 1896. This small box of dirt housed at the Smithsonian National Museum of Natural History (B28122) is enough to identify what soil type this pair of green kingfishers (*Chloroceryle americana*) thought was optimum on a bank of the Medina River, Texas.

incubators, maintaining a high internal temperature that is perfect for egg development. Utilizing these mounts results in an endless supply of nesting sites. Once the nest is vacated, the termite colony obliterates the opening and commences rebuilding the interior. The next breeding season, often the same pair excavates a fresh hole at precisely the same location. A pair of buff-breasted paradise kingfishers (*Tanysiptera sylvia*) used their favourite termitarium eight years in a row.[7] These nest holes are shallow, about 4 centimetres ($1^1/_2$ in.) in diameter and located approximately 50 centimetres (20 in.) off the ground in termite mounds, or higher if arboreal termitaria are utilized. Paradise kingfisher females often use their long central tail feathers as excavating tools to help sweep the dirt out of a burrow. In contrast, males hold their tails off the ground in a protective fashion, never risking damaging their magnificent tail feathers when excavating burrows.[8]

Excavating is still the rule of thumb for *Ceyx* Tree Kingfishers, but in what, and how deeply, is extremely variable. Several species burrow into termitaria, a few utilize abandoned tree cavities, and fewer still chisel away and make their own tree holes. Beach kingfishers like abandoned tree holes but are suspected of nesting in the fibrous crowns of coconut palms. The nesting habits of many of the rainforest recluses, the hard-to-find kingfishers, have never or rarely been observed and are either little known or completely unknown.

There are many bewildering reports of kingfishers deviating from the norm. These include laughing kookaburras and stork-billed kingfishers (*Pelargopsis capensis*) hammering into masonry, common kingfishers utilizing rabbit burrows, malachite kingfishers (*Corythornis cristatus*) breeding in aardvark burrows, and ruddy kingfishers (*Halcyon coromanda*) dwelling in the mud-clad exterior walls of houses and, once, in a hornet's nest.[9]

Arboreal and ground termitaria function as self-heating incubators. This illustration, based on a photograph by D. Le Souef, is of a buff-breasted paradise kingfisher (*Tanysipteras sylvia*) perched in front of its ground termitaria nest hole. A second paradise kingfisher is flying in the background.

Kingfisher eggs are white, more round than ovoid, and unremarkable. The typical six- to seven-egg clutch of a belted kingfisher is equivalent to between 37 and 52 per cent of a female's body weight. The rare clutches of eleven to fourteen eggs are speculated to occur when two female belted kingfishers utilize the same burrow.[10] Incubation lasts two to four weeks, with some adherence to the convention that smaller species take less time and larger ones take longer.

Female kingfishers lay one egg per day commencing a week after nest excavation is completed. During the egg-laying period, the couple spend most of their time away from the burrow feeding and living a non-parental lifestyle. Incubation begins when the last egg is laid. This delay results in hatching synchronicity,

Vog. v. N.I.   Uavogels. 15.

1.2. DACELO DEA. 3. D. SABRINA. 4. D. HYDROCHARIS.

Plate 15 from Hermann Schlegel's *The Birds of the Dutch East Indies* (1863–76) has a female common paradise kingfisher (*Tanysiptera galatea*) and two different aged fledglings at the top, showing how beak colour and tail length change with age. The bottom duo are adults in breeding plumage.

meaning that the chicks all hatch within twelve to eighteen hours of each other. Many birds do this, which is why a raft of ducklings or a peep of chicken chicks are so uniformly adorable.

Kingfisher chicks are both uglier and cuter than most nestlings. This oxymoron is the result of delayed feather maturation. The ugly-duckling stage is evident when they first extricate themselves from their eggs naked and blind, totally devoid of a fig-leaf covering of natal down. After hatching, belted kingfishers brood their young for a maximum of four to six days.[11] By day six, quill-like eruptions are visible on the chicks' backs. Each feather is surrounded by a waxy, usually grey, sheath. In most nestlings, these feather sheaths disintegrate rapidly, releasing the growing feather and resulting in chirping fuzzballs. Not so for kingfisher chicks: the persistence of these waxy sheaths for a protracted period inspires descriptors like 'hedgehog', 'porcupine' or 'pincushion' rather than 'fuzzy'. This is an ultra-comic, cute developmental stage, also seen in black-billed and yellow-billed cuckoos that brood their own chicks.

Retained feather sheaths possibly protect the feathers from fouling. Young kingfishers defecate on the walls of their nest chamber. When old enough, pied kingfisher chicks peck at the walls, enlarging the chamber but, more importantly, covering their faeces, thus resulting in a rough form of sanitation. This is not a universal behaviour. The norm is a faeces-filled nest.[12] Contributing to the stench and floor litter are regurgitated pellets containing fish, insect or crustacean indigestibles, plus trampled uneaten food. Definitely a nasty hole with oozy smells that a hobbit would abhor.

Though the inside of kingfisher burrows may be repugnant, the lack of general housekeeping does not deter from the theme of fidelity described in the 'Myth of the Halcyon'. Several behavioural studies do crack the perfection of Alcyone as the dutiful

Patterning eggs for camouflage purposes is unnecessary for cavity nesters. This clutch of plain white-belted kingfisher eggs (*Megaceryle alcyon*) housed at the Smithsonian National Museum of Natural History (B47649) are nearly spherical in shape.

wife and, by extension, the mother of the perfect family. Studies of the globally numerous pied kingfisher, one of the Water Kingfishers that reinvaded Africa and Asia, revealed alternative cohabitation arrangements. Studies conducted by Heinz-Ulrich Reyer of mating pairs in Uganda and Kenya found that one-third of chaste kingfisher couples were, in fact, trios. This threesome is always two males and one female. The extra male, or 'primary helper' as Reyer labels him, is commonly a yearling son of one (or both) of the breeding couple or, less frequently, is unrelated. During courtship, the primary helper participates in the noisy displays and ritual food-giving. More often than not, he gives his fish to the dominant male, who immediately gives it to the female. This dutiful son, or adopted brother, is a full member of the team. He excavates the burrow with the couple, develops a brood patch with which to incubate the eggs for part of the day and feeds the nestlings. It is at the nestling stage that one or two secondary helpers may augment the trio by giving fish to the female. At Lake Victoria sites, Reyer's studies calculated that nests with no helpers raised an average of 1.8 young, nests with one helper reared an average of 3.6 young, and nests with two helpers reared 4.7 young.[13]

Neville Cayley's 1892–3 watercolour depicts what was thought to be the norm for all tree-nesting birds: parents raising their young in isolation. The reality of laughing kookaburra mating systems is much more complex. Laughing kookaburras do nest in trees but also burrow into an eclectic variety of substrates.

Laughing kookaburra family units are more like community gangs, equally refuting the nuclear family Alcyone–Ceyx stereotype. Before courtship begins, rival breeding groups establish territories using two types of flight display purposefully performed at the intersection of territorial boundaries. In 'circle flight', one bird flies away from the group in a wide loop that intentionally crosses the boundary into the offending group's territory before circling back. Next, a kookaburra from the rival breeding group launches into the air duplicating this performance, and on it goes. Much more eye-catching are 'belly-flop' or 'trapeze' performances. The format is essentially the same except that mid-loop a single bird executes a flared landing on the edge of a potential nest site such as a tree hollow or, if there is no tree hollow available, pauses momentarily against a tree trunk before pushing off or belly-flopping away. In mid-flight, on the return trip to where its gang members are assembled, the kookaburra passes a teammate travelling in the opposite direction en route to replicate the same manoeuvre, hence the term 'trapeze territorial display'.[14]

The cooperative breeding system of the larger kookaburras is not only unique in the animal world, it is positively bizarre. Sarah Legge and colleagues discovered that in egg clutches, two-thirds of first-hatched eggs were boys, two-thirds of second-hatched eggs were girls, and the sex ratio of the third-hatched egg was at even odds. These findings suggest strongly that female kookaburras have an inherent mechanism to control the sex of their young. How is a mystery. Legge's study shows that the situation is even more complex because the make-up of the cooperative group altered the sex of the nestlings. Gangs with male helpers for the most part conformed to the above birth-order formula of male→female→either sex. But if female helpers are part of the cooperative breeding group, more male eggs are produced.[15]

All the laughing kookaburra groups studied avoided hatching a daughter first. The answer to this seemingly perplexing riddle is simple. Adult *Dacelo* sp. females are 15 per cent larger than their male counterparts. The large kookaburras start incubating the first egg as soon as it is laid, resulting in the young hatching asynchronously. In this scenario, the first chick hatches 24–72 hours before the second chick. If it is a female chick, she is inherently programmed to grow faster than a male chick, plus she has a one- or two-day head start at the feeding trough, making her significantly larger than the next hatchling. The male →female formula results in two chicks that are similar in size. The third nestling was killed in one-third of the nests within days of hatching as a result of aggression from its elder nestlings.[16] According to Legge, the variables necessary for 'kookaburra siblicide syndrome' are: (1) no male helpers attending the nest, resulting in fewer food deliveries; (2) the first and second nestlings to hatch are boy →girl; (3) there is a short hatch interval between the first two nestlings; and (4) the third-hatched nestling is much smaller than the second-hatched one.

Avian siblicide was first proposed by David Lank in 1954 as part of the 'brood reduction hypothesis'.[17] Reports of siblicide exist for boreal owls, barn owls, northern goshawks, blue-footed boobies and many other avian species where the young hatch on different days.[18] Competition for food results in fierce sibling competition: the biggest chick gets the lion's share of the food. If food is plentiful, most of the nestlings survive; if it is scarce, the youngest of the brood die and may become food for their siblings. Cainism, named after the fratricidal older son of Adam and Eve, is a variation on siblicide where only one chick survives. The killing of the second chick by the first-hatched Verreaux's eaglet happens in 90 per cent of nests studied, thus ensuring that the perpetrator gets all the food. While the parents are not directly involved, they do nothing to stop this murderous behaviour.[19] In 1962, E. F. Dorward proposed the now widely accepted 'insurance egg hypothesis', suggesting that the second redundant egg is laid as an insurance policy in case the first one is infertile or fails to hatch. The laying of a third egg by kookaburras can be viewed as an insurance egg in the event that one of the preceding eggs is infertile. Rarely do laughing kookaburras raise more than two chicks. The laying of an insurance egg plus the brood-reduction theory explains this behaviour, but it does not explain female kookaburras' apparent control of nestling gender and birth order.

Deviant animal behaviour skews our perception of the norm and is often over-represented in nature documentaries. The audacity of, not to mention the power implied by, female kookaburras having the capability to consciously or subconsciously determine what sex of chick goes in which egg is worthy of front-page headlines, not only for kingfisher-centric publications but for all those pertaining to the class Aves. The cooperative breeding systems of pied kingfishers and the larger kookaburras account for less than 1 per cent of this otherwise extremely conventional clan of birds. Linnaeus' assumption that Ovid's Ceyx and Alcyone were accurate models of kingfisher breeding fidelity is still the rule rather than the exception.

A larger threat to shattering the illusion of kingfishers as epitomes of peaceful family life happens when they communicate. Most kingfishers are noisy, restless birds who announce their movements with a shrill, discordant racket more suited to valkyries than chaste maidens. Belted kingfishers are aptly described as a 'rattle of kingfishers'; this epithet equally characterizes many kingfisher species around the globe. Not all birds can be songsters; kingfishers and many others do not have the equipment. The highly complex syrinx (avian vocal chords) of thrushes and nightingales is capable of producing multiple notes at the same time, resulting in complex melodies for which these most accomplished of oscine passerines are famed. Nor are kingfishers silent like stork, which use beak-clapping as an alternative.

The fiendish hyena-like call of the laughing kookaburra is the most outlandish and most famous of kingfisher vocalizations, so outlandish that it is part of the Hollywood tool kit – a voiceover for monkeys or used to add drama to a savage moment. An educated ear will discern kookaburras lurking within the soundtracks of *The Wizard of Oz* (1939), *The Treasure of the Sierra Madre* (1948), *The Swiss Family Robinson* (1960), *Count Dracula* (1970), *Raiders of the Lost Ark* (1981) and *The Lost World: Jurassic Park* (1997).[20] None of the localities of these movies are remotely near where laughing kookaburras actually live. Since *The Adventures of Priscilla, Queen of the Desert* (1994) is an Australian story, kookaburra calling is 100 per cent appropriate in this film, but it is likewise used to emphasize discord.

Some of the monikers for laughing kookaburras emphasize the humorous qualities of their raucous call: 'laughing jack', 'jackass' and 'ha-ha pigeon' to name a few.[21] The iconic laughing kookaburra song is composed of five phrases. The first three elements are 'kooa', 'cackle' and 'rolling'. The fourth element is 'ha-ha' or the laugh. The fifth and closing suffix is a sex-specific sound. Male songs terminate with 'go-go' while females finish their songs with a 'gurgle' flourish.[22] Laughing kookaburras are dawn and dusk choristers, plus on clear nights they are often heard serenading a full moon. If a discordant duet is heard, this signals that the breeding pair is unchaperoned. Kookaburras commonly roost at night in small groups, resulting in a protracted chorus. This more fiendish communal cry is created by the lack of synchronicity. Each bird starts and stops as it pleases. Wolf packs do something similar. The complex disharmonies created make it difficult for listening wolves to determine the size of a neighbouring pack.[23]

Normally the breeding male initiates the chorus. During the breeding season, kookaburra concerts are longer and louder, signalling that a territory is occupied. All birds must moult in order to replace their flight feathers; kookaburras do this in the post-breeding season and are the quietest at this time of slightly reduced flying ability.

When observing a riot of kookaburras, it is easy to single out who is talking. Vocalizing birds tilt their beaks skywards and cock their tails upwards – all in all a very clownish, oversized impersonation of wrens complete with rufous-barred tails. Kookaburra vocalizations convey information. A deep guttural 'kooa' on its own is a warning that a bird of prey has been spotted. An unaccompanied 'gurgle' signals the feeding of nestlings or announces a changing of the guard regarding incubating duties; squawks

The pied kingfisher (*Ceryle rudis*) on the right has a fish in its beak.

While in Tanzania, Peter Candido captured this image of a brown-hooded kingfisher (*Halcyon albiventris*) vocalizing.

emitted by adults indicate submission or a wish to be fed.[24] When fighting, screeching is the norm. Both laughing and blue-winged kookaburras (*Dacelo leachii*) occasionally shake their heads so violently that the two parts of their beaks clap against each other, producing a drumroll or rattling noise. The meaning of this call is unclear.

Though not as demoniacal, other halcyonid forest kingfishers (*Todiramphus macleayii*) utilize a dawn chorus to advertise their presence and delineate territories. Even the seldom-seen shovel-billed kingfisher can be reliably heard emitting three to four clear notes just after dawn. Hook-billed kingfishers are persistent vocal-izers, making short solitary calls at almost regular intervals. This is odd for a kingfisher on two counts: they are the only primarily nocturnal vocalizers in the clan, and hook-billed kingfishers are often heard calling incessantly for hours, sometimes all night long.

Many River Kingfishers species have only one call: a lone or repeated high-pitched 'zeeet' alarm or contact call. Kingfishers living along streams have to contend with white noise, non-stop low-frequency sounds generated by flowing water. Studies indicate that kingfisher vocalizations above 1.5 kHz are unaffected by white noise.[25] The higher-pitched pulsed call of many aquatic kingfishers is probably an adaptation enabling their voices to penetrate above this noisy background. Bucking the stereotypical River Kingfisher trend, the common kingfisher could almost be called a songster. It has in its repertoire seven variations of the river clans harsh 'tit-tit' alarm and contact call. In addition, the male, or both sexes, use a rich variety of whistles and warbles during courtship. In his *History of Animals*, Aristotle writes 'of the family of the halcyons or kingfishers . . . there are two varieties; one that sits on reeds and sings; and the other, larger of the two, is without a note'.[26] The former is very likely to be the common kingfisher; the identity of the larger species is uncertain, but it is most certainly not mute. None of the kingfisher clan are. The first sound common kingfisher chicks make is a plaintive 'peep', evolving to a loud purring 'uirr-uirr' food-begging call by the time they are ten days old, and metamorphosing into a harsh, growling 'gred-gred' by fledging time.[27]

Studies of nestling pied kingfishers' vocalizations also exhibit changes with age. This Water Kingfisher has complex social habits and a large repertoire to match. Its loud 'chickerker' is a territorial advertisement call. Aggression is denoted by a 'shreeur' call, plus there are several appeasement and begging calls. The standard contact call of the Water Kingfisher clan is 'tek-tek-tek' rather than the 'tit-tit' of the River Kingfishers.

Studies of the scream, the mew, the warbling call and the harsh rattle of belted kingfishers indicates that each has a distinct meaning. Counterintuitively, a belted-kingfisher scream indicates non-aggressive behaviour used in greeting a mate or when retreating from a threat. Males use a combination of a scream with a harsh rattle to attract females. After copulation, belted kingfisher couples emit mew calls and mew at each other while executing mock flying chases within their territories. Females warble to solicit copulation, and males occasionally warble while feeding older chicks. The well-known harsh rattle of this species is used in territorial disputes and when humans enter a pair's territory.[28] This harsh rattle consists of a series of single pulses. As aggression increases, more double or triple pulses are incorporated into the call.

Not all kingfishers are endless vocalizers. Nearing the top of a birdwatcher's or a researcher's frustration scale is locating maddeningly still, maddeningly silent kingfishers. Their habit of perching motionless in areas festooned with branches and vines within dimly lit rainforests makes spotting even spectacularly plumaged paradise kingfishers and some of the iridescent jewel-coloured kingfishers an exercise in patience. The noisy, extroverted nature of common kingfishers, belted kingfishers, pied kingfishers and laughing kookaburras makes them ideal behavioural research candidates. Their tolerance of humans invading their domain armed with binoculars, cameras, sound-recording equipment and clipboards has resulted in the collection of copious amounts of detailed data on their breeding and territorial behaviours, and especially about what and how they eat.

Being a carnivore with non-utilitarian feet, a kingfisher's beak must do all the work. Raptors often anchor prey beneath a foot and use their beaks to tear it into bite-sized pieces. In effect, their foot functions like a fork while their beak does the serious work

of being both a knife and a pair of pliers. Kingfishers, like all Coraciiformes, lack the stylohyoideus tongue muscle. Not having this retractor muscle greatly reduces tongue mobility and severely hampers food-processing abilities inside the mouth.[29] This handicap largely explains the characteristic food 'whacking' and 'smashing' behaviours of Coraciiformes. Snakes, lizards, amphibians, small mammals, birds, crustaceans, large insects and spiny fish are all laboriously clobbered, pummelled and pounded. This habit of softening, breaking internal bones and removing exterior hard parts by firmly gripping food with their substantial beaks while repeatedly beating the food against a branch or other hard surface is external food processing. When a food item is deemed 'done', customarily a head toss flings the now processed morsel up in the air so that it can be caught in such a manner that it goes

This photographic series by Charles J. Sharp documents a female giant kingfisher (*Megaceryle maxima*) whacking a tilapia, prior to swallowing it whole. This external food-processing removes spines or other sharp appendages that could become embedded in her throat.

In the event that a snake is bigger than its stomach, laughing kookaburras (*Dacelo novaeguineae*) swallow the snake's head first and let the remainder dangle out of their beaks until digestion makes room for the rest. The head of the snake is just visible, indicating that this bird has not partaken of its meal yet.

straight down the gullet, whole, with the head-end disappearing first. After the fact (and less elegantly), the indigestible bits – exoskeleton hard parts, bones, fur, feathers or scaled skin balls – are regurgitated as a bolus or pellet.

Despite being native to a relatively small and isolated subcontinent, the laughing kookaburra's zany laugh and snake-eating habits are globally well known. One laughing kookaburra study established that their diets are made up of 35 per cent lizards and snakes, 32 per cent insects, 15 per cent earthworms, 8 per cent crayfish, 1 per cent rodents and 7 per cent bird-table scraps.[30] Other studies state that kookaburras regularly eat frogs, adult and nestling birds, and metre-long (3-ft) venomous and non-venomous snakes. With a snake firmly clenched in its beak, a kookaburra purposefully flies skywards to gain elevation before dropping the snake onto hard ground to stun or kill it. A metre-long snake is too big for a 40-centimetre (16-in.) bird to swallow, but that does not stop these determined carnivores. Having consumed the head first, a kookaburra lets digestion take its course while the tail-end of the snake tail dangles in a most undignified fashion out of one side of its mouth.[31] Eventually digestion will make room for the rest.

Obligate carnivory is exhibited by even the Lilliputian members of the kingfisher clan. With great daring, Oriental dwarf kingfishers (*Ceyx erithacus*) fly at spider webs, aiming to pluck the resident spider off the web precisely at the same nanosecond that these kamikaze hunters execute a 90-degree evasive turn. A minor miscalculation and it is the bird that becomes the next meal of the intended victim, dwarf kingfishers not having the strength to disentangle themselves from ultra-sticky spiders' webs.[32] Equal in weight to a Pacific or winter wren, the African dwarf kingfisher (*Ispidina lecontei*) is the smallest of the clan. This diminutive insectivore feeds on damselflies, mantises, beetles, ants, large flies and other small insects. Within dark primary rainforests, dense riverine habitats, secondary forests or oil palm plantations, it silently perch-hunts 1 to 2 metres (3–6 ft) above the forest floor or sallies over water after flying insects. The standard food-harvesting strategy of kingfishers is this laissez-faire style. As a clan, they are perch hunters feasting on a smorgasbord of insects, crustaceans, small mammals, small birds and snakes. Anything that walks or slithers by is on the menu. Diving underwater is only part of the hunting repertoire of a select few.

Twenty or so kingfishers live up to the legend. These aquatic specialists actively fly to specific fishing spots and use their favourite perches as launchpads. Only a very few can actively hunt on the wing, usually by hovering. When these aerial hunters re-emerge from the water, their prize need not be a fish; it might be a crustacean, a tadpole or another aquatic denizen. Pied king-fishers are the most athletic hunters of the entire kingfisher clan.

With their wings held high, they let their bodies hang down vertically during brief bouts of hovering and rapid wing-beating, before diving after fish. Their shoulders are heavily muscled, and their pectoral muscles are slightly smaller than those of similar-sized birds.[33] This hover-hunting releases pied kingfishers from the dependence most kingfisher species have on perches for either aquatic or terrestrial hunting. Records exist of them hovering over water 3 kilometres (2 mi.) from the shore of Lake Kariba, Zimbabwe. Pied kingfishers have equally been spotted far out at sea. This athleticism includes the ability to eat small fish while on the wing, enabling them to carry on hunting without returning to land.[34]

Kingfishers living in the temperate regions of the western hemisphere by and large conform to the 'fisher' stereotype. Summer dietary-intake studies of common kingfishers reveal that fish comprise roughly 60 per cent of their diet. The remainder consists of aquatic insects, with the occasional mollusc or crustacean in the mix.[35] Belted kingfishers have more catholic tastes. They eat

This information panel at Jurong Bird Park, Singapore, includes dietary information about collared kingfishers (*Todiramphus chloris*).

the equivalent North American pescatarian diet of their European counterparts, plus frogs, salamanders, water shrews, young sparrow chicks and butterflies.[36] Records of both species eating the occasional berry in winter exist, but this is thought only to occur under duress during extreme food shortages.

As a rule of thumb, kingfishers do not migrate. Only the two northern-dwelling species, the common kingfisher and the belted kingfisher, are forced to migrate when their territories become frozen wastelands. Without extensive fat reserves or an ability to hibernate, they must eat 365 days of the year. In winter, flying and aquatic insects are dormant, and the birds' aquatic food sources are shielded by ice, thus reducing their culinary options. Seaside-dwelling North American belted kingfishers can ignore the harshest winter months, as do the crested kingfishers, who utilize the network of streams associated with the numerous hot springs on the island of Hokkaido, Japan. Common kingfishers are feeding specialists of gently moving streams or still waters; anything more than a veneer of ice and the consequence is starvation. Prolonged cold snaps result in steep population declines. In Britain, common kingfishers migrate no more than 250 kilometres (155 mi.). At the other extreme, common kingfishers breeding near the three great Siberian rivers (the Lena, the Ob and the Yenisei) migrate in excess of 3,000 kilometres (1,864 mi.). Food resources dictate that northern breeders perform the classical seasonal entrance and exodus of migratory birds. The search for an unoccupied, bountiful breeding territory where a pair can reign supreme to raise their young is what drives this system. The lack of winter food enforces the cycle. Like many small birds, common kingfishers are nocturnal migrants.[37]

The common kingfisher found in Britain has seven subspecies. They are dispersed throughout western Europe, extending over the Ural Mountains to the North Pacific and China Sea, and as

Only three species of kingfisher are regularly seen in snowy environments: common, belted and crested. Since only one of these species has a red beak, the stylized kingfisher at the centre of Kanu Tashun's 1700s painting, *Kingfisher and Snowy Bamboo*, is a common kingfisher (*Alcedo atthis*).

far east as Japan. Common kingfishers live on both sides of the equator, populating most of the islands of the South China Sea including those of Indonesia. Two subspecies live on the Australian side of Wallace's Line in Papua New Guinea and the Solomon Islands. They are currently under investigation and will probably be expelled from the *Alcedo atthis* clan and set up shop as *Alcedo hispidoides*, the cobalt-eared kingfishers. Despite this pending reduction in subspecies, the common kingfisher is, and will remain, the most widely distributed kingfisher species on the planet.

Laughing kookaburras are endemic to Queensland, New South Wales, plus a small portion of South Australia. This Aussie icon originally inhabited less than half of Australia. Deserts, tall mountain ranges, oceans or large expanses of water are all dispersal barriers for kookaburras. Laughing kookaburra populations in Perth, Western Australia, Kangaroo Island near Adelaide and throughout the Tasmanian archipelago, could not have been established without human 'help'. The beneficial reason extolled at the time was that laughing kookaburras would reduce venomous tiger snake populations. Further afield, laughing kookaburras were translocated to Auckland and Whangarei on New Zealand's North Island. In New Zealand feral laughing kookaburras are akin to vacuum cleaners. Rather than being helpful, they have become dangerous ecological pests, decimating native species that lack avoidance behaviours or adaptations against these formidable alien carnivores. This list of misdemeanours includes stealing the grub of unsuspecting tourists unaware that anything cooked or uncooked on a barbecue is fair game from a kookaburra's point of view.

The backdrop of Charlotte Montanaro's common kingfisher (*Alcedo atthis*) drawing is a map of all the countries where it is known to breed. This species has the largest range of all the kingfishers.

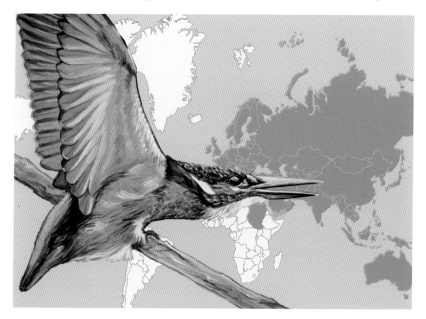

Another invasive species is responsible for having annihilated a kingfisher species. The Guam kingfisher (*Todiramphus cinnamomina*) was one of only eleven native forest birds on this North Pacific island. It is a run-of-the-mill Tree Kingfisher with a piercing 'breee-breee' call to contribute to the forest cacophony. Their heads are accented by a Zorro-esque ultra-thin black mask, which gives these cinnamon-headed kingfishers a mischievous air. Like all of their brethren, Guam kingfishers are ruthless carnivores, being especially fond of geckos and other small lizards. During the Second World War, brown tree snakes were accidentally translocated from the Solomon Islands to the u.s. naval base on Guam. Over time, the snakes disastrously altered the ecosystem by eating more than 300,000 birds on this 544-square-kilometre (210-sq.-mi.) island, thus eradicating the bird population. The silencing of Guam is horrific in the way that Alfred Hitchcock's film *The Birds* is bone-chilling. References to Rachel Carson's 1962 blockbuster book *Silent Spring* are inevitable. The sheer silence of Guam's tropical forest is menacing. Larry C. Shelton, leader of the Guam Bird Rescue Project and curator of birds at the Philadelphia Zoo, commented in 1986: 'It was the heavy silence. A dawn in the tropics without bird sounds bordered on the surreal. The silence was so complete that it seemed to be audible, and so eerie that I felt like shuddering.'[38]

Subsequent studies discovered that the island of Guam had the highest density of snakes on Earth, calculated as being four hundred times more numerous than a representative patch of the Amazon rainforest.[39] Protecting Guam's native forest birds was deemed impossible. Plans were made to rescue the five endemic birds, but the populations of three species had dwindled to such low numbers that they went virtually extinct before the programme started. Only the Guam rail and Guam kingfisher could be saved. The 'Great Guam Rescue' (equally dubbed

In 1914,
H. H. Calvert,
a prominent
Australian wildlife
artist, executed
this watercolour
of a laughing
kookaburra (*Dacelo
novaeguineae*)
holding a snake.

'Zoo East') resulted in 29 Guam kingfishers finding their way to American captive breeding facilities. In 1986 the Guam kingfisher Red List classification of 'Critically Endangered' was changed to 'Extinct in the Wild'. Fifty years after the kingfishers were airlifted out of Guam, the world population of Guam kingfishers oscillates between 145 and 160 birds living in 25 zoo and aquarium facilities.[40]

The current reality on Guam is that the snakes are still winning and there is no point in reintroducing kingfishers. Releasing them back into the wild is not just about saving one charismatic species. When Guam's forest once again resounds with 'breee-breee' kingfisher calls, this will herald a return to normalcy. The near absence

The Guam kingfisher (*Todiramphus cinnamoninus*), or Sihek, is one of Guam's five endemic birds. It is currently 'Extinct in the Wild'. The captive breeding population oscillates between 145 and 160 birds.

of forest birds and extreme reduction in the numbers of the Guam Mariana fruit bat and several of the endogenous geckos and lizards have resulted in a population explosion of spiders. The spiders are blanketing the landscape with webs. This high spider population is causing extinctions of butterflies and arthropod species. The cessation of avian, bat and arthropod pollination and seed dispersal has depleted plant biodiversity. It is not just Guam's animals that are fading away; the trees and plants are severely impacted too. If brown tree snakes can be eradicated, or brought under control, then bird, bat and lizard numbers will increase, allowing plant and insect imbalances to slowly rectify. Guam kingfishers are important pollinators of *Pisonia* trees, a cornerstone species of the island and a tree formerly used by kingfishers to rear their broods. While raising their chicks, Guam kingfishers used to inadvertently get sticky *Pisonia* seeds tangled in their feathers and transport them to other patches of the forest, thus completing the life cycle of this locally important tree.

The story of the stowaway that silenced Guam is currently part of the teaching syllabus about how one seemingly small change can drastically alter an entire ecosystem. All the island's endemic birds are either extinct or eking out an existence elsewhere. The Guam kingfisher is fortunate to be in the latter category. Sixteen other kingfisher species are in trouble, four of which are Critically Endangered (see Appendix II). A complete reversal of these accounts of kingfisher species in trouble is the havoc perpetrated by laughing kookaburras due to their purposeful introduction into ecosystems where they do not belong.

Though they are supreme predators, kingfishers are in turn predated upon. Their skulking behaviour when they sense danger reflects this. Depending on food preference, some kingfisher species live up to their former appellation of 'king-hunters', and for the two dozen or so that actually do eat fish, 'kingfishers' is an

Stork-billed kingfishers (*Pelargopsis capensis*) use their considerable beaks to grasp lizards and other bulky prey items.

appropriate term. Despite their oversized teddy-bear heads and outwardly pleasing demeanour, kingfishers are not friendly, nor as virtuous as they may seem. Water Kingfishers are more apt to bite than calmly inspect you if you have one in hand. From personal experience, a ringed kingfisher's bite hurts, plus they retain their hold with the tenacity of a bulldog. From chance observations of kingfishers stoically perched waiting for their next meal to come into view, it is easy to imbue all kingfishers with positive attributes based on their fine suits of clothing and obvious hunting prowess. It is more accurate to think of them as family-centric kamikaze killing machines.

3 Celestial Kingfishers

The boldness and flashy attire of kingfishers have not gone unnoticed, resulting in their being part of the cast of characters featured in myths, legends, folk tales and teaching stories around the globe. Kingfishers avoid extreme heights. Rather than inhabiting the skies, most of them execute short, purposeful flights and spend their lives in grasslands or the lower to mid-canopy of forests, or, if they have an affinity for water, hug the shorelines of rivers, lakes and oceans. Humans and kingfishers often co-exist within easy visual range of each other; they are part of our accessible natural heritage, and, if we so choose, we can visually participate in their everyday lives. Personality differences of regional species are reflected in how they are portrayed. Some are perceived as self-important, outspoken individuals, others as warriors and others still as retiring birds living in marital harmony.

Ovid's title 'The Myth of the Halcyon' alludes to the Mediterranean period of calm weather that occurs annually around the winter solstice. As per the Oxford Living Dictionaries, halcyon is derived from the Greek words *als* + *kuōn*, translating to *sea* + *conceiving*. The modern English usage of the word *halcyon* is either historical, denoting a period in the past that was idyllic and peaceful, or in the present, referring to a period of extremely good weather.

In the Greek pantheon, Alcyone is the granddaughter of Poseidon. Her father Aeolus is the ruler of the winds. He keeps them contained in a cave or possibly a rock tower. When directed by the gods, Aeolus plunges his sword into the rocks to release the appropriate wind. In depictions of 'The Myth of the Halcyon', Aeolus rarely figures, but his presence is alluded to by the inclusion of rugged rock formations or the illusion of a cave. One of the poignant images in Arthur Golding's 1567 translation of Ovid is of Alcyone on the shore looking in horror at Ceyx's drowned body as it floats towards her. The moment of avian transformation occurs the instant she takes action to kill herself:

Shee lept thereon . . .
   She flew, and with her new growen winges did beat
the ayre as tho.
   And on the waves a wretched bird shee whisked to
and fro.
   And with her crocking neb then growen to slender bill
and round,
   Like one that wayld and moorned still shee made a
moaning sound.
   Howbee't as soone as she did touch his dumb and
bloodless flesh,
   And has embraast his loved limbes with winges made
new and fresh,

. . . through compassion of the Goddes both hee and shee
   Were turnd to birdes. The love of them eeke subject to
their fate,
   Continued after: neyther did the faythfull bond abate
   Of wedlock in them being birdes: but standes in
stedfast state.[1]

The colouring of this Oriental dwarf kingfisher (*Ceyx erithaca*) is exquisite.

Richard Wilson's *Ceyx and Alcyone* painting (1768) depicts Alcyone distraught as the corpse of her drowned husband, Ceyx, is hauled out of the sea. When directed by the gods, Aeolus, Alcyone's father, must unleash winds, waves and thunder stored in the sea cave depicted on the right.

Most authors portray the pair as romantic innocents, but the plight of Alcyone and Ceyx is also told as a cautionary tale of wrongdoers getting their just deserts. Romantic versions start with the devoted couple reluctantly saying goodbye before Ceyx departs on a sea voyage to consult an oracle timed to take advantage of the traditionally calm seas of mid-winter. Every day that he is away, his dutiful wife lays out a suit of his clothing as a talisman to bring him safely home. Drowning, especially if the body is lost at sea, was particularly feared by the ancient Greeks. Without a proper land burial, a person was unable to travel to Hades and thus denied a resting place for their soul. Taking pity on Alcyone, Hera, the queen of immortals, sends Morpheus, the god of dreams, to inform her that Ceyx is dead. Upon waking Alcyone rushes to the shore to find the drowned body of her beloved husband. The gods are so moved by her grief that first she, and then Ceyx, are transformed into kingfishers. In volume one of his 1955 *Greek Myths*, Robert Graves recounts a much sterner tale. The married couple is so blissfully happy that they childishly liken themselves to Olympians, with Alcyone daring to call herself Hera, and her husband Ceyx, Zeus. In anger at this affront, the gods release a thunderstorm which destroys Ceyx's ship. The ghost and dream messenger in the Graves version is no other than

This illustration by Antonio Tempesta depicts Morpheus, the god of dreams, telling Alcyone that Ceyx is dead. Through the window, Alcyone is portrayed subsequently finding her drowned husband on the shore.

110.   *Morpheus Ceycis corpus Halcyoni repreſentat.*

Ceyx himself: 'His ghost appeared to Alcyone who, greatly against her will, had stayed behind in Trachis, whereupon distraught with grief, she leapt into the sea. Some pitying god transformed them both into kingfishers.'[2]

Aristotle published *History of Animals* three hundred years before Ovid incorporated his section on kingfisher breeding behaviour into 'The Myth of the Halcyon'. In *History of Animals* Aristotle fancifully describes the kingfisher's nest this way:

> Its nest is like sea balls, the things that go by the name of sea foam . . . The color of the nest is light red and the shape is that of the long-necked gourd. The nests are longer than the largest sponge, though they vary in size, they are roofed over and a greater part of them is solid and a greater part hollow . . . It is not known for certain of what material the nest is constructed; it is possibly made of the backbones of the gar-fish; for, by the way, the bird lives on fish.[3]

Obviously, Aristotle never witnessed common kingfishers excavating burrows in riverbanks nor did he see them going in or out of real nest holes. In 'The Myth of the Halcyon', Ovid is equally unaware that common kingfishers nest in burrows.

The ancient Egyptian word *qrr.t* either means a cavern of the underworld, a hole in the earth, or a nest burrow of either a kingfisher or a bank swallow.[4] The etymology of *qrr.t* suggests a link between the nesting burrows of these two birds and the underworld. Possibly the burrows were thought of as conduits for people to traverse between the two worlds.

The American Arikara (Missouri River Basin) creation myth starts in a post-apocalyptic dark universe where everyone is living underground. The Mother of the People, known as Corn Mother, leads everyone out of this dark underworld by digging a hole. She is aided first by Badger, then by Mole and finally by Mouse, who is the first to break through. Mouse is blinded and retreats back to the underworld. Corn Mother enlarges the hole, allowing all the animals (including birds) to come with her out of the darkness. She goes on to lead her people westwards with Kingfisher pointing the way, Owl guiding them through the dark forest and Loon leading them across the lake.[5] Another variation has everyone except Kingfisher trapped underground. By relentlessly flying at the riverbank, Kingfisher collapses the bank, liberating Corn Mother and all the creatures.[6]

Australian Aboriginal creation myths have a dark universe as their starting point. What comes next varies but usually begins with the spirits deciding that the birds and beasts are unhappy living in the dark. One account has a god-spirit throwing an emu egg high into the sky. As the egg shatters, the yolk ignites, setting a bonfire ablaze and thus illuminating the world. More typically, the sky spirit(s) and laughing kookaburra forge a partnership. One variation has it that when the kookaburra calls at dawn, the sky spirit turns his wheel to bring out the sun.[7] More commonly, the sky spirits band together to collect wood and stack it so high that they can no longer see the top of the pile. When they set it ablaze, light and warmth come into the world. Daily, the Morning Star announces the impending lighting of the woodpile. But few creatures take notice of the Morning Star and are perpetually startled when the light comes. To solve this problem, a council is convened to decide which animal should be appointed the world's morning trumpeter. As the spirits deliberate, they hear a most amazing sound and go to investigate. A kookaburra has launched itself from its perch and pounced on a mouse. After conquering his prey, the bird started to laugh and laugh and laugh. Impressed by this happy sound, the spirits ask the laughing kookaburra to be the morning trumpeter. Realizing that this would make him a hero, respected and important, the kookaburra accepts the job of waking all the sleeping creatures before the spirits light their bonfire each morning. Later, when the Creator brings people into the world, the spirits tell the people, 'You must never tease kookaburra . . . If kookaburra hears you making fun of him, he will never laugh again. Then we will no longer have light or warmth.'[8]

Probably originating from East Anglia (UK), this 1480s illumination depicts Noah's Ark. In accordance with the biblical text, both a raven and a dove are released from the ship to seek land.

In the Bay of Bengal, the extremely remote Andaman archipelago is the home of a culture that lived in substantial isolation from 200 BCE until the eighteenth century. Despite this, and in keeping with many other peoples around the globe, the Andamanese have a flood creation myth. In it, a common kingfisher plays a beneficial role. The occupants of a canoe have the good fortune to be out at sea when the mighty waters come. Upon returning home, the two men and two women are devastated by the sight of the ruined landscape and the eradication of their kinsmen. In the form of a kingfisher, a deceased friend appears and sees that they have no fire. Up in the sky, Puluga, the Creator, is seated by his hearth. Boldly the kingfisher sneaks beside the Creator and seizes a burning log, places it on his back and attempts to fly off. However, the log slips off the bird's back, hitting Puluga. In a fury, Puluga hurls it at the bold little kingfisher. The burning log misses the bird and falls down to Earth. Most fortuitously, it lands at the very spot where the four fireless ones are deploring their fate.[9]

The *Epic of Gilgamesh* contains the first written account of a 'Great Deluge'. This part of the epic centres around Utnapishtim, who is instructed to build a great boat called 'Preserver of Life'. The Gilgamesh flood saga includes a raven and a dove deployed as 'living compasses' after the storm abates. When at sea, doves can detect land up to 35 kilometres (22 mi.) away and, when released, instinctively orientate themselves towards the closest shoreline. According to Genesis 8:9, after the storms had abated Noah sent forth first a raven, who never returned, and then doves, one of whom returned with an olive branch.

The more mischievous tales of what happened when Noah released a kingfisher are not chronicled in the Bible. A British West Country version has it that when the common kingfisher finally remembers that he must tell Noah that he found land, the ark has long since been dismantled and turned into houses. To this day, kingfishers are still searching for the ark, which is why they fly low, hither and thither along rivers, calling for their master.[10] In another tale, a despondent grey-plumaged common kingfisher is so relieved after his confinement in the ark that, when Noah releases him, he is dazzled by the sun and flies straight towards it. The bird flies so high that his back takes on the blue of the sky. As he approaches the sun, its heat scorches his breast, forcing the bird to turn around and dive into the water to douse his smouldering feathers.[11] Alternatively, the common kingfisher's burnished-orange breast feathers are stained by the sun's glow.[12] What happens next in these folk stories and sagas when the kingfisher remembers the task Noah charged him with is highly variable. One narration has Noah refusing to let the disobedient, self-satisfied bird with his beautiful new appearance live inside the ark; this is postulated as the reason why common kingfishers only live near water.[13] Another version, pertaining to the belted kingfisher, has Noah so irritated that he makes the bird stay out on the deck. He refuses to feed the kingfisher, forcing the bird to fish for its own food from the surrounding water.[14] In this tale, the belted kingfisher usually has a rufous belly band, which by default means she is a female. Male belted kingfishers have no rufous feathers.

Globally there are multiple stories explaining kingfisher colouration. South American Arawak storytellers relate that the ringed kingfisher and the grey-winged trumpeter quarrelled over the spoils of war. They knocked each other into the ashes, which accounts for their grey plumage.[15]

Dorothy Tanner's book *Legends from the Red Man's Forest* (1895) includes a vignette called 'The White Spot of the Kingfisher', which explains two aspects of a belted kingfisher's attire:

The Ojibwe trickster Manabozho [alternatively called Nanabush] is worried about one of his dearest friends. He

In her 1916 book *Bird Neighbors*, Neltje Blanchan wrote: 'The noon day heat of an August day that silences nearly every other voice, seems to give to the indigo birds [belted kingfisher (*Megaceryle alcyon*)] only fresh animation and timbre.'

asks the kingfisher who knows about everything under water to find out why the man drowned. Kingfisher informs him that the serpents have taken his friend to their home. Manabozho thanks the kingfisher by hanging a metal of wampum on his neck – it is the white spot you always see on the breast of a belted kingfisher. Manabozho then has a change of heart and catches kingfisher with the aim of killing him to prevent the serpents from knowing that he is hunting for his friend. Kingfisher slips out of his grasp but his long head feathers have been so ruffled by Manabozho's rough handling that they have never since been smooth.[16]

British botanist and ornithologist Mark Catesby playfully reminds his early 1700s audience that this New World kingfisher is indeed a 'fisher' by inserting a piscivore in the bird's beak. The posture of this female belted kingfisher (*Megaceryle alcyon*) is incorrect.

Another version of this story agrees that Manabozho rewarded the kingfisher with a white medal for useful information. Immediately after bestowing this kind gift, Manabozho turned on the kingfisher, wringing the bird's neck, which is why to this day kingfishers have a white collar and ruffled head feathers.[17]

The Jicorilla of the Apache Nation have a saga called 'The Fox and the Kingfisher'. One segment is about Fox and Kêt-la'-i-le-ti

(Kingfisher) meeting and deciding to go to the kingfisher's house. When they arrive, Kêt-la'-i-le-ti says, 'I have no food to offer you.' Fox watches the kingfisher dive through 15 centimetres (6 in.) of river ice, catch two fish and cook them. The two friends enjoy their meal so much that fox invites Kêt-la'-i-le-ti to his house.

When Kêt-la'-i-le-ti arrives at Fox's house, Fox says, 'I have no food to offer you.' Fox goes down to the river and leaps from the high bank. Instead of plunging through the ice, he breaks his head and kills himself. Kêt-la'-i-le-ti goes to him, catches him up by the tail and, swinging him around four times, restores him to life. Then the kingfisher plunges through the ice and catches some fish. 'I am a medicine man,' Kêt-la'-i-le-ti states. 'That is why I can do these things. You must never try to catch fish in that way again.'[18] A Sioux variation of this story has Ictinike, the son of the Sun God, diving into the river for fish to feed his wife's grandfather, the kingfisher. Likewise, the kingfisher comes to the rescue, preventing his grandson from drowning.

Raven rattles used by the North American West Coast nations of the Haida, Tlingit and Tsimshian are powerful icons of spiritual transformation. The man on the raven's back can be a shaman invoking the guidance of the spirits, or, alternatively, the raven is transporting a dead person's spirit. Via a red tongue-bridge, the man and the frog are united, symbolizing divine assistance to the shaman, or, alternately, the tongue-bridge is a lifeline as the person is transported to the afterlife.[19] If the kingfisher is part of the shaman–frog tongue-bridge, the kingfisher is part of the partnership providing divine assistance. If the kingfisher is facing backwards or not connected to the others via the tongue-bridge, the kingfisher represents death.

In several cultures, kingfishers are associated with fighting. In the Ramayana, Hanuman the Monkey King thwarts the demon's moves in the Assamese legend 'The Slaying of Mahiravana' by

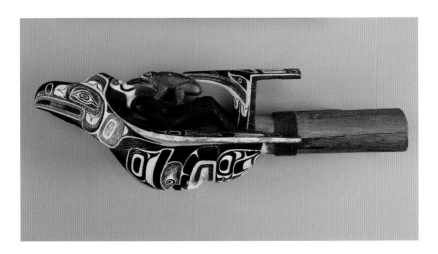

On the back of this Kwakwaka'wakw raven rattle the shaman is united to his source of supernatural power, the frog, by a tongue through which the magic force flows. The red paint inside the kingfisher's beak emphasizes that this bird's tongue is equally joined to those of the frog and the shaman.

successively transforming himself into a crow, a kingfisher, a fly, an aged Brahman, a crow again, a second fly and the vampiric goddess Vetalacandi.[20] For the Dusun people of Sabah, Borneo, regardless of the direction of its flight, warriors on the way to battle who see a *Mantis Raa* (thought to be an Oriental dwarf kingfisher) must return home immediately or face serious illness. Seeing an *Embuas* (banded kingfisher) is a favourable omen for the Iban people of Sarawak, Borneo, especially if it calls to the right-hand side of the person who hears it.[21]

In many Southwest Pacific island cultures, kingfishers are the incarnation of the gods of war or other deities. The European names of 'sacred kingfisher' and '*Todiramphus sanctus*' honour this belief. One of Captain James Cook's men, Georg Forster, shot several sacred kingfishers on the island of Huahine. Captain Cook was warned by the Tahitians not to continue killing kingfishers, who were *Atua*, or supernatural beings.[22] On another island later in the voyage, the shooting of sacred kingfishers soured relations between the Europeans and the Society Islanders. Captain Cook noted that Forster should have known better than to shoot three kingfishers since he had already been warned on Huahine. When Cook met with Reo, the Bora Bora Regent of Ra'iatea, to ease tensions, one of the daughters 'wept to see the sacred birds dead. Reo told them very solemnly not to kill any more kingfishers and herons on his island.'[23]

Taeme, one of many Polynesian gods' names, means 'glittering black'. Only under the right light conditions do the iridescent blue-black feathers running down the back of sacred kingfishers

This watercolour by J. Georg Forster was executed while on board HMS *Resolution* during Captain Cook's second expedition to the South Pacific. Forster shot several of these sacred kingfishers (*Todiramphus sanctus*), causing diplomatic tensions with Pacific Islanders.

emit dazzling black flashes. On the Samoan island of Upolu, *Sa fulu sa*, the name of the kingfisher war god, translates as 'of the sacred feather'. If *Sa fulu sa*, the endemic flat-billed kingfisher (*Todiramphus recurvisrostris*; formerly *T. sanctus recurvisrostris*), flies in advance of a Samoan war party, it is an omen of victory. If *Sa fulu sa* flies towards the warriors as they are preparing for war, this signifies defeat.[24]

The Māori of New Zealand revere *kōtares'* (*Todiramphus sanctus vagans*) watchful sentry behaviour. For long periods of time, *kōtare* perches motionless, then attacks its prey in a blur of motion. The elevated platform in a Māori *pā* (fort), which is used to watch for enemies, is sometimes referred to as a *kōtare*.[25] Māori warriors admire the sacred kingfisher's tremendous self-control and lightning speed when it is time to strike.

Globally, celestial kingfishers are minor deities with limited magical powers or are minor characters in shamanistic rituals. Only in a few parts of the South Pacific and Melanesia have they been elevated to the rank of gods, usually war gods. The importance of celestial kingfishers in local mythology and teaching stories in part mirrors the visibility, daily habits and outward appearance of local kingfisher species. The timing and joyous call of laughing kookaburras, and their perceived self-importance, have understandably resulted in them being assigned the task of awakening the world each morning. Overall, kingfisher and kookaburra portrayals, whether as minor deities or folkloric heroes, are helpful and demonstrate exemplary behaviour.

4 Bejewelled Kingfishers

The Chinese art form of *tian-tsui* resembles cloisonné, but, instead of enamel, it utilizes the magnificent iridescent blue feathers many kingfishers possess. Probably starting in the Qin dynasty (221–207 BCE), the rank of nobles determined how much *tian-tsui* ornamentation they were permitted to wear. Conveying prestige, kingfisher-feather items were especially coveted by brides seeking *fengguan*, phoenix bridal crowns of the highest quality. The refrain of a poem by Ch'en Zi-ang (661–702 CE) reflects on this greed:

> The halcyon kingfisher nests in the South Sea realm
> Cock and hen in groves of jeweled trees
> How could they know that the thoughts of lovely women
> Covet them as highly as yellow gold?[1]

Tian-tsui created from feathers plucked from kingfishers, imported alive from what is now Cambodia, were deemed to be of the very highest quality. This live bird and feather trade was a major economic pillar of the Khmer Empire, helping to fund the building of Angkor Wat.

The most common English rendering of the traditional Cantonese and Mandarin characters 點翠 is *tian-tsui*, usually translated as 'dotting with kingfisher feathers'. The best pinyin or phonetic interpretation is *dian cui*. Looking at the characters more closely, the first character, *dian*, means 'mark'. The second character, *cui*, is a chrononym – a word that denotes a colour and an animal, in this case 'deep blue' and 'halcyon'.[2]

The skeletal framework of *tian-tsui* is the same as cloisonné. Silver or a similar metal is shaped into the desired object, then silver or gold wires are affixed to form compartments, or *cloisons*. In cloisonné, each compartment is subsequently filled with enamel, sometimes augmented by inserting perfectly fitted glass or gemstones into some of the partitions. In *tian-tsui* objects, the blue infill consists of iridescent kingfisher feather barbs.

In the annals of Emperor Da of Wu (courtesy name Zhongmou), a 235 BCE entry states that pearls, halcyon (kingfisher) feathers and tortoiseshell were given in exchange for horses from the northern state of Wei. Records from 137 BCE document that King Nanyue gave Emperor Wen a thousand pairs of kingfisher plumes and eighty live kingfishers as tribute.[3] The utilization of feathers as

Manchu women attending festivals and ceremonies often wore these distinctive wedge-shaped *tian-tsui* headdresses made of black silk gauze or netting adorned with kingfisher feather ornaments. Many of these intricate *tian-tsui* pieces had elements suspended from wires which swayed slightly when the wearer moved her head.

tribute payments was not restricted to Asia. Formerly, Hawaiian commoners were obliged to give the highly prized yellow rump feathers of the Hawaii mamo to their sovereign; items of feathered regalia cost thousands of avian lives.[4]

A constant in ancient Chinese portraiture is the depiction of royal blue or turquoise elements in court hats, wedding head-dresses, phoenix crowns and less formal hair ornaments. All these depictions of blue or turquoise elements are assumed to be *tian-tsui*. Over millennia and across geographic regions, Chinese wedding, court and everyday attire varied tremendously. The wearing of phoenix crowns probably originated during the Tang dynasty (618–907 CE). Many breathtaking, excellently preserved phoenix crowns from the Ming dynasty (1368–1644 CE) still exist.

Some of the oldest and most spectacular *tian-tsui* masterpieces that have survived the centuries are hats and coronets. Court hats denoted rank and social prestige. Overall lavishness, type of fur trim, and size and type of gems followed strict imperial protocols. Only the court hats of emperors, empresses and top-ranking consorts could include depictions of dragons and phoenixes. Golden

Intricate hairpins denoted status and adulthood. Strict rules determined how many a woman was allowed to wear. Young girls before the age of puberty were not allowed to wear hairpins.

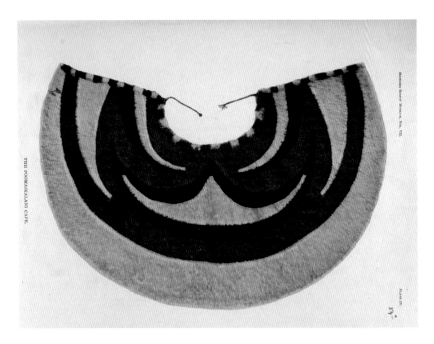

PLATE IV.

Thousands of bird lives are sometimes required to make a feather cape. In this Hawaiian example the feathers are from small passerines, the red feathers are *'i'iwi* and the yellow and black feathers are *'ō'ō*. This cape is 1 metre wide.

pheasants denoted imperial princesses. On their wedding day, brides of wealthy families wore elaborate headdresses typically with a curtain of pearls hiding the bride's face. These prized heirloom wedding headdresses were supplied by the groom's family. If no suitable bridal headdress was available, it was the groom's responsibility to purchase one.[5] The custom of storing wedding headdresses, court hats and coronets in specially built boxes in part explains why so many of these heirlooms have survived.

The complexity and abundance of *tian-tsui* pre-date the eighth-century CE writings of the Tang emperor Xuanzong, but his book, *Rules of Costume*, helps us understand their importance and why there is such an abundance of *tian-tsui*. The work includes a section devoted exclusively to hairpins. In summary:

The empress should wear twelve hairpins, each with a decorative head.

As woman's social status declines, the number of hairpins is reduced.

The face of a Cantonese bride wearing this style of headdress is partially obscured by the veil of pearls. The groom's family is obliged to supply the bridal headdress, which is commonly a family heirloom.

Mythical Chinese phoenixes embody the five human qualities of virtue, duty, ritually correct behaviour, humanity and reliability. They could only be worn by emperors, empresses and top-ranking consorts. This phoenix is one small element in a headdress thought to have been worn by the empress dowager Cixi, the last effective ruler of China.

Hairpins cannot be worn before a woman reaches adulthood.

Images of the dragon and phoenix in gold can be enjoyed only by direct family members of the emperor.[6]

Phoenixes in Chinese art should not be confused with the desert-dwelling European mythological bird that, after burning on a funeral pyre, rises rejuvenated from the ashes. Mythical Chinese phoenixes embody five human qualities, the conventional interpretation of which is that the head symbolizes virtue, the wings represent duty, the back is ritually correct behaviour, the breast humanity and the stomach reliability.[7]

Many black-and-white and tinted photographs record how prevalent kingfisher adornments were in the nineteenth century and at the beginning of the twentieth. The preferred demeanour of wealthy Han Chinese women, often with diminutive lotus feet, was to appear small and fragile while their Manchu counterparts favoured tall headdresses and 10- to 15-centimetre-high (4–6-in.) platform shoes, both of which accentuated their height. Manchu headdresses, especially those of the gate-tower *liang-patou* style, showcased detachable *tian-tsui* accent pieces. The structural element of a *liang-patou* headdress is a latticework armature of wire (iron or copper) or rattan covered in black silk, gauze or thread netting, or foliate strips of satin. Fresh flowers, *tian-tsui* and other medallions are then affixed to this bat-like superstructure. This ornamentation was likewise incorporated into the headband-style headdresses worn by Han women.

John Thomson's photograph of Manchu women (*c.* 1898) documents their elaborate hair styles.

Tian-tsui three-dimensional ornaments are highly complex. Every layer or suspended element is an intricate work of art complementing the central design. Some parts are dainty and pendulous, soldered onto coils of wire designed to move with the wearer. More often than not, each element is inlaid with kingfisher feathers.

Small *tian-tsui* jewellery pieces and hairpins are not rare. They can be purchased on eBay and other Internet sites and in antique shops. If you were a wearer of *tian-tsui* at the turn of the nineteenth century, chances are you had a lot of it, and, being prized, it was well cared for and carefully handed down to the next generation. Globally, contemporary Chinese opera companies treasure their inventory of sumptuous *tian-tsui* theatrical head-dresses, phoenix crowns, court-official hats, hairpins and jewellery required for staging authentic traditional Cantonese operas.

Manchu women often wore their hair up under a bat-like *liang-patou*. These flat, folded, angled headdress of black silk on a metal frame are worn parallel to the shoulders. On this framework *tian-tsui* and other types of ornaments were attached. When appropriate, fresh flowers were added, giving additional height to the wearer.

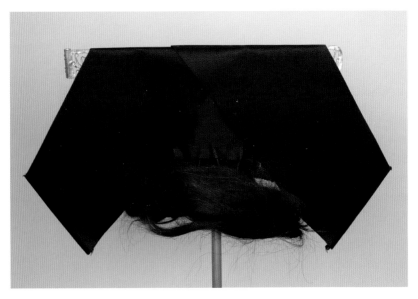

In her memoir *Mrs Marco Polo Remembers*, Mary Parker Dunning recounts her 1908 round-the-world honeymoon. She describes her fascination with *tian-tsui*:

> We watched breathlessly the making of kingfisher feather jewelry . . . You get one of the bird's wings if you buy a pin, so that the world outside of China will believe it. I bought a kingfisher pin. The foundation of the pin is cheap silver. Then the wonder worker, a patient, spectacled Chinaman takes a single hair from out of the bird's wing, draws it through a bit of glue and lays it on the silver foundation, then another hair, which he lays beside the first, then another and another and another, endlessly and head achingly and eye-tiringly, until he has laid the filaments from the feather of the bird's wing so closely together that they look like a piece of enamel.[8]

Dunning does not name the kingfisher species, but a different passage in the book suggests it was akin to the white-throated kingfisher or perhaps its less valuable cousin, the black-capped kingfisher (*Halcyon pileata*). Both these species have the spectacular blue iridescent wing panels she noted, making them such memorable souvenirs.

Though descriptive, 'hair' and 'filament' are not correct feather terminology; Dunning is using familiar words metaphorically to refer to feather barbs. Barbs are strands of keratin with hook-and-eye structures that, when zipped together, amalgamate into feather vanes. *Tian-tsui* craftsmen pluck one or more barbs, making sure a minute part of the feather shaft remains to keep the barbs from disintegrating.[9] This feather-barb segment is trimmed to the desired length and, as aptly described by Dunning, is drawn through warm glue before it is affixed within a *cloison* onto the base metal. In *Kingfisher Blue: Treasures of an Ancient Chinese Art* (2001), Beverly Jackson extensively researched the composition of this glue. As well as a superlative adhesive on metal, it must not alter feather iridescence or sheen, plus it must be truly invisible, drying crystal clear. Over the millennia, many glue recipes specifically formulated for *tian-tsui* consisted of, but were not limited to, seaweed, animal hides and especially fish bladders from bottom-feeders (carp, sturgeon, catfish or cod). Like animal hide, fish bladders contain collagen, which, when rendered, yields a clear adhesive.

Initially *tian-tsui* was reserved for members of the Chinese imperial court, but over the centuries this filtered down to the aristocratic strata of society. Tai san-krai (Great New Street), Canton, was the *tian-tsui* manufacturing epicentre in the nineteenth century. This district was visited by many Western tourists who, like Dunning, wished to purchase or witness this ancient art form. Chinese immigrants also established a *tian-tsui* manufacturing enclave in San Francisco, California.

Ostrich, bird of paradise, raptor, duck, pheasant, peacock, chicken and other spectacular – or even characterless and ordinary – feathers are used worldwide for self-adornment. What is it about blue kingfisher feathers that inspired a unique art form that lasted for over two millennia? Why was it limited to so few kingfisher species? All over the world and in Southeast Asia, kingfishers come in a myriad of hues. Many species, like the Oriental dwarf kingfisher, have no blue feathers and are never used in *tian-tsui*, while the brilliant blue, kingfisher-esque feathers of another member of the Coraciiformes, the Indian roller, are occasionally used. Interestingly, these very same rollers have vibrant violet feathers frequently used in *tian-tsui* landscape panels and other decorative arts, but these violet hues are never included in pieces for personal adornment.[10] What was the compelling factor that resulted in the use of these brilliantly blue- and turquoise-hued feathers in the production of decorative panels, hair ornaments, brooches and especially the headdresses and coronets worn by Chinese royalty, high-ranking officials, wealthy women, brides and opera singers?

Zhan Ziquian, a mid- to late sixth-century painter, is credited with formulating the 'blue-green style' of Chinese landscape painting. Beverly Jackson's theory is that his peaked mountains rendered in malachite green and azurite blue, gently rolling away and oozing partway down their sides with stark, narrow black outlines, influenced generations of Chinese painters, and eventually led to the creation of landscape panels using kingfisher feathers.[11]

Many kingfisher species have the magnificent iridescent wing feathers used for fabrication of *tian-tsui* pieces. Black-capped kingfisher are one of many *Halcyon* species used.

Before modern times, sources for the manufacturing of blue paint for artistic applications were limited. Ground-up lapis lazuli or cobalt oxide compounds were the most common raw materials for blue pigments, ceramic glazes or enamels. Utilizing blue kingfisher feathers was an alternate way to create pure blue fields of colour.

No bird possesses blue-pigmented feathers. The blue we observe in birds' feathers is an optical illusion referred to as 'structural colouration'. The blue we think we perceive in 'blue birds' or a stray blue feather we find by chance on the ground appears blue due to nanostructures within the feather. Like a blue sky or the surface of a calm lake or tranquil ocean, this optical effect (Rayleigh scattering) results in the human eye perceiving short-wavelength light scattering off oxygen and nitrogen molecules as 'blue'. Several mechanisms exist that cause blue structural colouration with or without iridescence in birds. Unlike classical iridescence, which is caused by light reflecting off minute differences in tissue densities, the presences of ultra-microscopic air vacuoles (bubbles) just beneath the surface of feather barbs interferes with visible light. When light strikes these vacuoles embedded in the β-keratin feather matrix, blue short-wavelength light is reflected.[12] In blue-crowned manakins (*Lepidothrix coronata*) and indigo buntings (*Passerina cyanea*), the spherical air vacuoles in the keratin-layer array resembles Swiss cheese composed of more air than cheese. The organization of the hollow, cylindrical air vacuoles in the β-keratin matrix of blue-hued kingfishers and corvids does not look like anything in particular, more of a blurred jumble of white and dark shapes.

Depending on the exact wavelength reflected, a feather appears to the human eye as violet, royal blue or turquoise. If no light illuminates a blue feather, it is actually black. Similarly, if you grind a blue feather using a mortar and pestle, the result is a dark powder. Grinding red northern cardinal or red English robin feathers results in a red or rust-coloured powder due to the carotenoid pigments that give these feathers their red and red-orange hues. The spectacular blue kingfisher feathers used for *tian-tsui* were never

Xu Yang's *Palace of the Immortals* is a much more recent work utilizing the 'blue-green' landscape style of painting. He painted this folding fan in 1753.

The feathers of this albino malachite kingfisher (*Corythornis cristatus*) have the same microstructures as feathers that reflect short-wavelength blue light, but without any melanin present in the feathers as a backdrop, all light is reflected, resulting in the bird appearing white.

ground or modified in any way. More the reverse: they had to be handled with care in order not to damage or scratch them. Once scratched, a dark mark blemishes a feather for eternity because the matrix of minute air vacuoles has been irrevocably damaged. Never again will it reflect blue light.

Père David, a Catholic Lazarist missionary-priest, botanist and zoologist who spent many years in China, is best remembered for returning home to Paris with a giant panda pelt, the first ever seen by Europeans. *Les Oiseaux de la Chine*, the 1887 bird atlas he co-authored, contains one of the earliest Western accounts of how *tian-tsui* feathers were obtained: 'In South East China these birds [kingfishers] are netted in large numbers, their captors pluck the back feathers, which they use in making the well-known king-fisher jewelry, then release the birds.' In the original French, a

sympathetic Père David notes, 'doit être sinon très-douloureuse, au moins fort désagréable pour les martins-pécheurs' ([it] must be very painful, at least very unpleasant, for the kingfishers).[13] The harvesting of only the back feathers points to the common kingfisher, which has iridescent blue feathers restricted to the back and upper tail region. Père David called the bird *Alcedo bengalensis*. This species was originally described in 1788, thirty years after Linnaeus described the common kingfisher. It had full species rank when Père David was writing. In the intervening centuries, this bird was downgraded, becoming a subspecies of the common kingfisher (*Alcedo atthis bengalensis*). Another common name for it is 'Indian small blue kingfisher'. Though extensively used, this is not the most prized or sought-after species of kingfisher for the fabrication of *tian-tsui* objects.

Southern coastal China and the adjacent tropical countries are the home of the ne plus ultra *tian-tsui* kingfisher, *Halcyon smyrnensis*. This kingfisher has two English names: the ioc World Bird List (see Appendix 1) calls it the white-throated kingfisher, but it is equally known as the white-breasted kingfisher. The back, upper tail feathers and wings of this species are an extraordinary, brilliant deep blue-green. An anonymous Chinese writer described it as 'vying in color with the sky and blue-green neutral tints of the distant hills'.[14] In his essay 'The Vermilion Bird' (1984), Edward Schafer points out a problem with the English appellation of this bird 'whose common name does not reveal that its head and belly are maroon and that its back shines with iridescent cobalt and glinting turquoise'.[15] A thirteenth-century account describes how to catch these birds by stealth. The hunter would crouch in the foliage near a pool of water favoured by kingfishers, 'with a small net in hand: near him stands a cage, in which he has put a female kingfisher, in order to attract the male. The man waits till the bird approaches and then captures him with the net. Sometimes he takes four or five of them in a morning, sometimes not a single one the whole day.'[16]

In his book *The Civilization of Angkor* (2001), Charles Higham suggests that as early as the first Khmer delta state (150–550 CE) there existed a 'far-flung trading network extending westward to India, Persia and the Roman empire and northeast to China' which included perishable exports such as feathers, spices, fabrics and wood. The Khmer capital was moved to Angkor in 802 CE and persisted there until it was sacked and abandoned after the

In China, Père David encountered this subspecies of common kingfisher, *Alcedo atthis bengalensis*. Ambient lighting alters the appearance of iridescent feathers. In this photograph, the feathers running down the back and tail of this kingfisher glow with a life of their own.

For the manufacturing of *tian-tsui,* the ne plus ultra bird was the white-throated kingfisher (*Halcyon smyrnensis*). The blue iridescent feathers of these kingfishers were once coveted by royalty, high-ranking officials, brides and all those that copied imperial styles. These birds were economically valuable and widely traded.

1431 Thai invasion.[17] At one time Angkor was the most populous city of antiquity, with an estimated population of 700,000 to one million people.[18] Angkor Wat tops the list as the largest religious structure in the *Guinness Book of Records*. This complex of 72 major monuments extends over 24.8 kilometres (15.4 mi.) and covers an area of 1,626 square kilometres (approx. 628 sq. mi.). The 190-metre-wide (623-ft) moat that surrounds the 3.6 kilo-metres (2.2 mi.) of outer walls is a significant aquatic ecosystem that provides feeding and nesting habitat for kingfishers.

The British writer Osbert Sitwell, visiting as a tourist in 1949, described Angkor Wat as a water civilization:

We need no longer be surprised at the extent of the artificial lakes, the number of pools and moats and basins or at the existence of the water-gardens and pleasances of Angkor Wat . . . for over all of them dipped, skimmed and flashed then – as still to the present – the most exquisite kingfishers; larger and with a more vivid tint of green, sea-green and lime-green and jade-green, than you can find anywhere else in the world . . . These feathers . . . combined all the elements, the blue of the sky, the green of the jungle, the fiery gold of the sun. For once these jeweled plumes have been transmuted by magic of art into another medium, into something as beautiful as themselves but less transient.[19]

When this thriving metropolis was at its zenith, Zhou Daguan (known in French as Tcheuo Ta-Kauan) lived in Angkor from 1296 to 1297 CE. Zhou was part of an official diplomatic delegation sent there by the Yuan Emperor Temür Khan, the grandson of Kublai Khan. Other than the inscriptions that survive on Angkor buildings, Zhou's book *The Customs of Cambodia* is the only existing chronicle of everyday life in ancient Angkor. He reported that Khmer royalty imported pewter, lacquer trays, blue porcelain, mercury, vermillion, paper, sulfur, saltpetre, sandalwood, orris-root, musk, canvas, cloth, umbrellas, iron pots, copper utensils, oils, wooden combs, needles and various kinds of Chinese matting. In turn, the Khmer traded beeswax, bird feathers, rhinoceros horn and other tropical-forest products.[20] Adrien von Ferscht writes:

The finest kingfisher feathers were to be had from Cambodia and were prized above all. The export trade of feathers to China was one of the largest export earners for the Khmer empire and was used to fund the construction of many magnificent temples, including Angkor Wat. The mass slaughter of the kingfisher in Cambodia led not only to the species becoming almost extinct but it is believed to have contributed considerably to the decline of the Khmer Empire itself when demand could no longer be met.[21]

John Tully, author of *A Short History of Cambodia* (2005), thinks the 'charming Khmer tale which held that Angkor fell into decline because the supply of kingfisher feathers ran out' is absurd, but agrees with Bernard-Philippe Groslier and Roland Fletcher that ecological damage may have been a factor in the civilization's decline.[22] Fletcher had postulated that Angkor's growing population resulted in 'a vast consumption of timber . . . for the scaffolding of the temples [and] for building the palaces and houses'.[23] Add to this the demand for wood as cooking fuel for its 700,000-plus inhabitants. The deforestation of the Kulen Hills north of the Khmer capital probably led to soil erosion, silting of watercourses and possibly a reduction of oxygen in the water due to eutrophication processes. This in turn would have had a negative impact on fish and other aquatic invertebrate populations dependent on the rice paddies and other watercourses, thereby greatly reducing kingfisher habitat, food and nesting sites. Tully suggests that if Fletcher's theory is correct, the fate of Angkor is a lesson for modern Cambodia and the rest of the world.

The habitat loss in Cambodia has resulted in sharp declines in tigers, crocodiles and other animals, and appears to be a rerun of the habitat loss that ended the kingfisher-feather trade with China and heralded the decline of Angkor. Tully suggests that the Angkor legend of the kingfisher is a parable:

damage to the ecosystem of Angkor might well have first manifested itself in the disappearance of the birds. It was

Angkor Wat, one of many temples in the city of Angkor, honours the Hindu god Vishnu. In the early 1200s, Suryavaran II built this enormous temple symbolizing the mythic Mt. Meru. The temple's five inter-nested rectangular walls and moats represent chains of mountains and the cosmic ocean.

probably greed for the revenue generated from kingfishers that resulted in it being noticed by the Khmer ruling class that the extensive aquatic ecosystem which surrounds Angkor had deteriorated. With no scientific explanation for this, the Khmers might well have regarded the disappearance of the birds as a harbinger of doom.[24]

The Khmer civilization based in Angkor and the American island of Guam are past and recent examples of what can go horribly wrong ecologically. In both cases, humans inadvertently altered their environment, and the associated kingfisher was, or still is, a symbol of those environmental disasters. In both Angkor and Guam, kingfishers were part of nature's early warning system.

The Chinese art form of *tian-tsui* was in vogue for approx-imately 2,200 years, ending in the early 1900s – almost four hundred years after the Thai invasion of Angkor. It was the Boxer Rebellion, or Yihetuan Movement, that sounded the death knell for *tian-tsui* and eventually toppled imperial rule in China. Throughout her years in power (1861–1908) either as regent or adviser, Empress Dowager Cixi wore decadent court attire and commissioned many exquisite and extremely lavish *tian-tsui* headdresses and jewellery pieces. She was a lover of finery and had a vast collection of *tian-tsui*. In the final decades

Empress Dowager Cixi (1835–1908) probably owned this headdress. The small phoenixes emerging from the surface represent the empress, while the countless pearls and gemstones denote the high rank of the wearer.

of 'dotting with kingfisher feathers' fabrication, this glorious art form probably reached its zenith, attaining new heights of complexity. The abdication of the last Qing emperor in 1912 ended the need for court regalia. *Tian-tsui* quickly lost favour with the middle and upper classes as they severed all ties with imperial rule. Not wearing kingfisher jewellery in public signified one's cooperation with the new government and rejection of the old order.

5 Influential Kingfishers

Even if it were possible to subtract or eliminate all the language, metaphors and illusions generated by Ovid's 'The Myth of the Halcyon' in the English language, kingfishers would still be seen to have influenced European thinkers, writers, poets, musicians and artists in innumerable ways. Historically, the Anglophone experience is based on only a very few kingfisher species. In the past, and to this day, common kingfishers have had a plethora of roles in art and literature. They are weather predictors, birds of omens, and the muses for poets and intellectuals.

Contemplating the mutability of species led Darwin to formulate his theory of evolution, which irrevocably changed the direction of literary and scientific thought. Though not pivotal, evidence exists that from the very beginning of his voyage on HMS *Beagle,* his observations and ruminations about kingfishers played a small role in the development of his theories of evolution and sexual selection. Only four kingfishers are listed in Clifford B. Frith's lengthy book *Charles Darwin's Life with Birds: His Complete Ornithology*. Frith discusses three collected by Darwin in South America: a green kingfisher (*Chloroceryle Americana*) shot in Argentina in 1833, and two ringed kingfishers (*Megaceryle torquata*) shot in Uruguay in 1833 and in Chile a year later. All three specimens are currently 'missing', but there is very good documentation that they did in fact exist. There is no disputing the existence of

Charles Darwin collected this grey-headed kingfisher (*Halcyon leucocephala*) on Sao Tiago Island, Cape Verde during his voyage on HMS *Beagle*. It resides at the Natural History Museum at Tring, England.

the grey-headed kingfisher collected in January 1832 at Porto Praia, Santiago Island, Cape Verde Islands. This round study skin specimen resides in the Natural History Museum, Tring (NHMUK 1881.5.1.3018). Tied to its legs is a label stating that it was collected by C. Darwin, Esq.

Darwin's observations on grey-headed kingfishers form the first ornithological account published in his *Journal of Researches into the Natural History and Geology of the Countries Visited During the Voyage of ʜᴍs Beagle*. On page two, he states:

> The commonest bird is a kingfisher *Dacelo iagoenis* [now *Halcyon leucocephala acteon*] which tamely sits on the branches of the castor oil plant and thence darts on the grasshoppers and lizards. It is brightly coloured, but not so beautiful as the European species: in its flight, manners and place of habitation, which is generally in the driest valleys, there is also a wide difference.[1]

This bird marks Darwin's first observation that island species behave differently from continental species. Tameness is not universal but a very common characteristic of isolated island-dwelling reptiles, birds and sometimes mammals, a subject that Darwin was to write much about in future years. His awareness of the unique nature of island archipelagos began a mere 22 days after he left England. Despite the Galápagos attracting most of the limelight as the crucible of evolutionary thought, this grey-headed kingfisher reference from the Cape Verde archipelago suggest that Darwin was musing about the uniqueness of island fauna three years before reaching the Galápagos.

Did Darwin collect a kingfisher when he was in the Galápagos? In the Cambridge Darwin Archives, in Darwin's own handwriting, there is a list of all his Galápagos birds classified by John Gould, curator of the Zoological Society of London's museum. The first bird on this sheet of paper is the Galápagos hawk; then various predatory birds are listed, including a kingfisher. Today, belted kingfishers are the only resident kingfishers found in the Galápagos, making it a safe bet that this was the species Darwin saw and possibly collected.[2] At the Zoological Society of London meeting held on 24 January 1837, Gould presented six new species of predatory birds from Darwin's Galápagos collection, one of which was a 'hitherto unknown species of kingfisher'.[3] At this point the scent goes cold on two fronts. The belted kingfisher had been described by Linnaeus as *Alcedo alcyon* in 1758, ruling out the possibility of Gould writing it up as a legitimate new species in 1837. This alleged Galápagos kingfisher skin or skeleton has no surviving illustration, and any additional notes by Darwin or Gould are either lost or never existed. Despite a document in Darwin's own handwriting, and the existence of a reference in the Zoological Society of London archives stating that Gould presented information on it, it is highly unlikely that Darwin collected a kingfisher from the Galápagos. These kingfisher notations by him and by Gould are now viewed as errors.[4]

After the HMS *Beagle* adventure, Darwin started to lead a double life. Outwardly he was a clubbable young naturalist on the rise. While awaiting the publication of his manuscript *The Voyage of the Beagle,* he secured funding from Her Majesty's Treasury to be the editor of a multi-volume compendium – *The Zoology of the Voyage of HMS Beagle* – and outwardly became consumed with this large undertaking.[5] Secretly, however, he was scribbling in his transmutation notebooks, collecting, questioning and developing his theory of evolution. Kingfishers come up several times. As Darwin pondered the mechanics of transmutation, how inheritance works and if species could change, he noted that one of the *Alcedo* kingfishers residing in the Moluccas scarcely differed from its European counterpart and asked, 'Was having a sharper, slightly longer beak enough to divide kingfishers living half a world apart into two species or were they merely varieties?'[6] The naturalist Alfred Russel Wallace was pondering and writing about the same evolutionary questions at the same time. In a letter addressed to Wallace dated 23 February 1867, Darwin wrote, 'When next in London, I must get you to show me your kingfishers.'[7] Two months later, in a letter dated 29 April, he noted, 'When we met at the Zoological Society and I asked you about the sexual differences in kingfishers, I had this subject in view, as I had when I suggested to [Henry Walter] Bates the difficulty about gaudy caterpillars which you have so admirably, as I believe it will prove, explained.'[8]

In *The Descent of Man* (1879), Darwin uses the eating habits of kingfishers to support what he termed 'a habitual and purposeless movement'. Kingfishers living in aviaries, he observes, continue to beat their meal against a stout branch (in theory to kill or stun it), even though it means the loss of their meal, as happens when ground meat is bird-handled in this manner.[9] Likewise, Darwin suggests that the foot-pattering of the ground by kagus, common shelducks and flamingos when zookeepers approach with food is a recreation of the foot-dancing done by these species to mechanically force worms up to the surface of waterlogged soils. Along with many other examples, Darwin thought such behaviours were acquired by natural selection.

Western thinking started to waver when Wallace and Darwin jointly presented their ideas on speciation; it changed irrevocably in 1859, when Darwin published *On the Origin of Species*, followed two decades later by *The Descent of Man*. Prior to this, Pythagoras, Plato, Newton and legions of other thinkers had been essentialist, believing that the diversity of the world emphasized its invariance and stability. There was a limited number of natural essences (kinds or types), each forming a class. The members of each class were thought to be identical, constant and sharply separated from the members of other essences. An example often used to illustrate this concept is: 'There exists a wide variety of triangles but a triangle can never be a quadrangle.'[10] Equally, a raven can never be a kingfisher. This typological thinking had an impact on everything; anything that deviated from the norm was an abnormality.

This plate by John Gerrard Keulemans from the 1892 *Catalogue of the Birds in the British Museum*, vol. XVII, illustrates the differences between three subspecies of the blue-breasted kingfisher (*Halcyon malimbica*) – considered full species at the time of drawing.

Charles Darwin encountered grey-headed kingfishers (*Halcyon leucocephala*) in the Cape Verde Islands 22 days after leaving England on HMS *Beagle*. This kingfisher species is the topic of his very first ornithological observation while on the voyage.

J. G. Keulemans del. et lith.   Mintern Bros. Chromo lith.

1. *Halcyon armstrongi* .   2. *Halcyon solomonensis* .
3. *Halcyon chloris* .

The importance of a supreme being – a creator – to explain the existence of these types, or essences, was essential to understanding the reasons for stratified human society and diversity in nature up to and during most of the Victorian era. As in the example about geometric shapes, Victorian essentialists thought that 'natural essences' indisputably separated people of different skin colour into static classes. Darwinian thinking shattered this mindset. It shattered the concept that life, including human life, is predestined or dictated by a supreme being.

The eventual acceptance by the majority of philosophers, writers and citizens of the theory of evolution – that life forms, including humans, change – had far-reaching consequences. The minor differences among common kingfishers living worlds apart that had perplexed Darwin at first are examples that life is not static, not preordained. Speciation is not part of a grand plan. It was no longer irreverent to think or publish ideas detached from theology.

Sigmund Freud's protégé Carl Gustav Jung had a dream mentor whom he called Philemon. In January 1914 Jung was writing and illustrating his *Red Book* and was on the verge of completing a dream-image of Philemon as an old man holding four keys. Happenstance resulted in Jung finding a dead kingfisher while walking in the garden of his lakeshore home. 'I was thunderstruck,' he wrote, 'for kingfishers are quite rare in the vicinity of Zürich, and I had never since found a dead one.'[11] Shortly thereafter, Jung added kingfisher-coloured wings to his Philemon painting. The finding of a dead kingfisher added a means of flight to a dream image Jung had formerly depicted flying unaided.

Possibly drawing on Jung or the discipline of psychoanalysis for inspiration, American humourist James Thurber wrote the following parable for his *Further Fables of Our Time* series originally published weekly in *New Yorker* magazine. In Thurber's

The bhagavad gita says: whenever there is a decline of the law and an increase of iniquity, then i put forth myself. For the rescue of the pious And for the destruction of the childers /for the establishment of the law i am born in every age.

ΠΡΟΦΗΤΩΝ ΠΑΤΗΡ ΠΟΛΥΦΙΛΟΣ ΦΙΛΗΜΩΝ

Ich gehe meine straße weiter, ein feingeschliffen, in zehn feuern gehärtet stahl, im gewande geboren, ist mein beglei- le ein panzerhemd

liegt mir um die brust, heimlich unterm mantel getragen. über nacht gewann ich die schlange lieb und habe ihr rätsel errathen. ich setze mich zu ihr auf die heißen steine am wege. ich weiß sie listig und grausam zu fangen, jene kalte teufel, die den ahnungslosen in die ferse stechen. ich bin ihr freund geworden und blase ihr eine mildtönende flöte. meine höhle aber schmücke ich mit ihren schillernden häuten. wie ich so meinen weg dahinschritt, da kam ich zu einem rötlichen fels, darauf lag eine große buntschillernde schlange. da ich nun beim großen ΦΙΛΗΜΩΝ die magie gelernt hatte, so holte ich meine flöte hervor und blies ihr ein süßes zauberlied vor, das sie glauben machte, sie sei meine seele. als sie genügend bezaubert war,

Die Schwalbe und der Eisvogel.

extremely short 'The Kingfisher and the Phoebe', Dr Kingfisher, the bird psychologist, examines Mother Phoebe's son, who refuses to sing anything other than 'phoebe'. (Before continuing with Thurber's fable, it must be remembered that phoebes are one of a long list of birds named onomatopoeically. Their name duplicates their most frequent call; the same is true of chickadees.) In this case, the errant son refuses to sing anything except 'phoebe, phoebe', much to Mother Phoebe's displeasure. Dr Kingfisher tells her, 'This phoebe is a phoebe like any other phoebe.' Mother Phoebe refutes the psychologist, saying that her son 'will take the place of the eagle on the dollar, or the canary in the gilded cage or the cuckoo in the cuckoo clock. You just wait'. Typical of this literary form, each of Thurber's fables concludes with a moral.

The moral of 'The Kingfisher and the Phoebe' is: 'You can't make anything out of cookie dough except cookies.'[12]

Other than featuring a kingfisher, there is no connection between Thurber's 'The Kingfisher and the Phoebe' fable and Aesop's sombre 'The Kingfisher' fable:

A kingfisher had carefully built its nest in a bank by the riverside so that it might be out of reach of the Fowler [bird hunter]. One day, while it happened to be away seeking for

Sir Edward Linley Sambourne, *Kingfisher*, late 19th century, ink and wash. The work is a clever pun that equates the prowess of English fishermen with that of kingfishers.

food for its young ones, the river suddenly rose and with great rapidity washed away the nest, young ones and all. On her return, the kingfisher, when she saw what had happened, exclaimed, 'Unhappy creature that I am! I fly from the mere thought of one enemy only to be destroyed by another!'

The Moral: Many a man, in providing against one danger, falls into another.[13]

Poets, playwrights and storytellers use metaphors to incorporate images and add double meanings and complexity while economizing on the number of words required. In one of his first poems, *The Book of the Duchess*, Geoffrey Chaucer enhances the love of John of Gaunt for his recently deceased wife Blanche of Lancaster by weaving in the marital bliss, subsequent tragedy, and transformations of Alcyone and Ceyx into kingfishers. Chaucer's story is one of the first English publications to allude to 'The Myth of the Halcyon'. Since then, innumerable love stories, mysteries, science fiction, poems and songs have been published with either minor or major references to kingfishers or 'The Myth of the Halcyon'. The French singer Jérôme Fagnet (known as Broken Back) omitted the word 'kingfisher' from his 2016 song 'Halcyon Birds'. In the refrain, he uses the title phrase to good effect as a romantic allusion.

John Milton's reference to kingfishers in 'On the Morning of Christ's Nativity' is much more political. Two stanzas focus on the absence of war. The beginning and concluding three lines of this passage are:

No war or battle's sound
Was heard the world around;
the idle spear and shield were high unhung;

. . .
Whispering new joys to the mild ocean,
Who now hath quite forgot to rave,
While birds of calm sit brooding on the charmed wave.

Milton wrote this poem in 1629, when two facts linked kingfishers with the Stuart monarchy. It was then common to use 'The Myth of the Halcyon' or the 'season of peace' to allude to the absence of war. Four years previously, Charles I of England had ascended the throne. It was still remembered that his father, James I, had kept a kingfisher as a pet.[14]

Perhaps due to Ovid, perhaps due to personal observations, kingfishers inspired poets to write poems simply titled '(The) Kingfisher'. The opening sentence of Scottish poet Norman Mac-Caig's 'Kingfisher' is akin to a breath of fresh air: 'That kingfisher jewelling upstream seems to leave a streak of itself in the bright air.' More about that certain something in the air than the bird itself, Walt Whitman equally used the kingfisher–halcyon days metaphor to conjure up a feeling. First published in the 29 January 1888 edition of the *New York Herald* newspaper, his short poem 'Halcyon Days' was later revised and published in Whitman's 1888 *November Boughs* book as part of the *Sands at Seventy* collection of poems.[15] In the ninth edition of *Leaves of Grass* (1891–2), this same collection of poems was added as an appendix. Whitman never revised the concluding lines of 'Halcyon Days':

As the days take on a mellower light, and the
apple at last hangs really finished and
indolent ripe on the tree,
Then for the teeming quietest, happiest days of all!
The brooding and blissful halcyon days!

'As kingfishers catch fire, dragonflies draw flame' is both the title and the opening line of a sonnet by Gerard Manley Hopkins, published in 1918, thirty years after his death:

> As kingfishers catch fire, dragonflies draw flame;
> As tumbling over rim in roundy wells
> Stones ring; like each tucked sting tells, each hung bell's
> Bow swung finds tongue to fling out broad its name . . .

The beauty of the phrase 'As kingfishers catch fire' resulted in its use as a title of many books and articles on Hopkins, in addition to publications on unrelated topics. Eugene H. Peterson's book of that name is about Christian religious spirituality, while Alex Preston's book, beautifully illustrated by Neil Gower, is a fusion of ornithology, literary anthology and partial autobiography.[16]

A kingfisher's mutability is often used as a tool to convey the meaning of life in passionate surrender to the spirit of change.[17] Amy Clampitt's 1983 book of collected poems *The Kingfisher* won her a 'Genius' grant – a MacArthur Fellowship – at the age of 63. This poem, set in New York, describes a kingfisher wandering the streets of the metropolis in November surrounded by the chaos of urban living. The concluding verse is:

> a kingfisher's burnished plunge, the color
> of felicity afire, come glancing like an arrow
> through landscapes of untended memory . . .

Shortly after American poet Charles Olson published his influential manifesto on 'projective verse', he wrote 'The Kingfishers'. This 1953 poem exemplifies his theory that verse should focus on 'certain laws and possibilities of the breath, of the breathing of the man who writes as well as of his listening'. Projective verse as per Olson is governed by two halves: 'The HEAD, by way to the EAR, to the SYLLABLE / The HEART, by way of the BREATH, to the LINE'.[18] Olson's 'The Kingfishers' sheds light on the vanity of the perfection of European civilization and the deterioration of the glory of ancient cultures at the hands of Western conquerors. It reflects on history using a philosopher's pen. The principal section alluding to kingfishers is midway through the poem. The iconic opening line is included in this extract:

> What does not change / is the will to change
> . . .
> Otherwise? Yes, Fernand, who had talked lispingly of Albers & Angkor Vat.
> . . .
> in some crack of the ruins. That it should have been he who said, 'The kingfishers!
> who cares
> for their feathers
> now?'
> . . .
> he repeated and repeated, could not go beyond his thought
> 'The pool the kingfishers' feathers were wealth why did the export stop?'

Later in the poem, Olsen states:

> The legends are
> legends. Dead, hung up indoors, the kingfisher
> will not indicate a favoring wind,
> or avert the thunderbolt. Nor, by its nesting,
> still the waters, with the new year, for seven days.

It is true, it does nest with the opening year, but not on
the waters . . .

This long, thought-provoking poem bordered on revolutionary
for its time for both its content and its style of writing. Not surprisingly, it spawned many technical papers and several books.
Here, we are only interested in Olson's kingfisher imagery. Ovid's
'The Myth of the Halcyon' pervades the poem and needs no retell-
ing. The lines 'dead, hung up indoors, the kingfisher / will not
indicate a favoring wind, / or avert the thunderbolt' start with a
folk-wisdom reference and end by either invoking Alcyone's father
Aeolus, the keeper of the winds, or a reference to Sir Thomas
Browne's, *Pseudodoxia Epidemica* (1646–72), on the properties of
kingfishers. Olsen need not necessarily have been well versed in
kingfisher folk wisdom if he had read Shakespeare's *King Lear*. In
Act II, Scene 2, the Earl of Kent speaks of those who 'Renege, affirm
and turn their halcyon beaks / With every gale and vary of their
masters'. These lines refer to the practice of using kingfishers as
weathercocks. Starting in the Middle Ages and continuing into the
twentieth century, it was thought by some that a mummified kingfisher hung by its beak from a string attached to the rafters of a
house could predict the weather, the beak indicating the direction
from which the wind was about to blow.[19] English and French sail-
ors hung kingfisher weathervanes in the rigging of their ships.[20]
Curious about the attributed occult and secret property of kingfishers as an indicator of 'winddrift', Browne experimented with
multiple kingfishers and discovered that each suspended bird
pointed in a different direction. Despite his publishing conclusive
proof that suspended kingfishers do not predict the weather, his
findings went unheeded and the practice continued.[21]

  Bird-based superstitions abound. Even in Victorian times,
wearing or having peacock feathers indoors was believed to be

unlucky. The evil eye – the ocellus on a peacock feather – has been, and is still, blamed for cursing numerous plays. Even today it is considered bad luck in some theatres. In contrast, wearing king-fisher feathers indoors was thought to be positive and to heighten the wearer's beauty.[22] Browne proposed 'that its [a kingfisher's] dried body kept in a house protected against lightning and kept moths out of garments'.[23] He was also convinced that dead king-fishers do not decompose. Four hundred years earlier, chronicler Giraldus Cambrensis, who tended towards the fantastical, had written:

> It is remarkable in these little birds that, if they are preserved in a dry place, when dead, they never decay and if they are put among clothes or other articles they pre-serve them from the moth and give them a pleasant odour. What is still more wonderful, if, when dead, they are hung up by their beaks in a dry situation, they change their plum-age each year as if they were restored to life, as though the vital spark still survived and vegetated through some mysterious remains of its energy.[24]

This extract from *Topographia Hibernica* (usually referred to as *The Topography of Ireland*) is from 'Chapter XIII – Of Martinets and Their Natures'. Martinets are described by Giraldus as 'less than the blackbirds, and here, as elsewhere, rare, frequenting the rivers. They are short like quails, and dive in the water after the small fish on which they feed.' A footnote gives two spellings – '*martinet* or *martineta*' – and reminds the reader that kingfishers are called *martinet-pêcheur* in French.

Today, the colloquial French name for *Alcedo atthis* is *martin-pêcheur d'Europe*, derived from the timing of St Martin's Day. The Feast of St Martin, *Martinstag* or Martinmas, falls on 11 November.

Historically this was the beginning of natural winter. 'St Martin's days' also alludes to a period of calm or of good weather in the fall or winter, referred to in English as 'Indian summer' or 'halcyon days'. In Shakespeare's *Henry VI, Part 1*, Act 1, Scene 2, Joan La Pucelle (Joan of Arc) tells Charles, the Dauphin of France:

Assign'd am I to be the English scourge.
This night the siege assuredly I'll raise:
Expect Saint Martin's summer, halcyon days,
Since I have entered into these wars.

The title of this late 1660s Flemish etching by Albert Flamen is *Alcedo: Martin-pescheur*, combining the genus name with the French common name for kingfishers.

In a totally different undertaking, the Arthurian quest for the Holy Grail, a different kind of 'fisher' is important. Percival (or Parsifal) and his companions go several times to the castle of the Fisher King, the keeper of the Holy Grail. On the first visit, all the knights fail to ask 'The Question'. The termination of their quest is dependent on someone asking why there is a procession every night. Why are a lance, a candelabra and a grail paraded through the dining hall of the Fisher King? How this is rectified

Alcedo: Martin-pescheur. *B. Flamen fe.*

– the lineage of the Fisher King, the nature of the evil spell on his kingdom, the entourage travelling with Percival, and the powers of the Holy Grail – varies with the interpretation. As a symbol of impotency, the Fisher King is always wounded and may, or may not, be capable of walking. He passes his enforced idleness fishing in the castle moat or nearby river, presumably in the company of, or being observed by, a *Kyngys fyschare* (Middle English for 'kingfisher').

A lone kingfisher is a different kind of observer in Hieronymus Bosch's triptych *The Garden of Earthly Delights*, which teems with imaginary creatures and unexpected groupings. The parables in these Netherlandish paintings from the late 1400s were understood by its Renaissance viewers. Each panel is an allegory. The first depicts humans in a tranquil earthly paradise. The largest, central panel depicts Bosch's fanciful vision of the present, of humans feasting on every pleasure, unconcerned about the consequences of their unchaste lives. The horrors of Hell are depicted in the third panel. There is an odd grouping of birds at the water's edge near the left border of the central panel. Half buried in this flock is a mallard drake with its head outstretched transporting an odd assemblage of passengers away from the group. In the Middle Ages, ducks were symbols of stupidity and alcoholism. The man riding the duck is assumed to be inebriated, therefore in no condition to realize that his seducer is evil, represented stereotypically for the times as a black woman. This fall from grace is observed by an oversized kingfisher. The kingfisher's disapproving demeanour looms large. Why the kingfisher is present, and what its role is, is unclear.

Kingfishers, along with a silent chorus of other birds, often symbolize abundance in art. In several ancient Egyptian masterpieces, they are depicted in profile, as are most animals and human figures from this time. A stone relief from the mortuary

'Kings-fisher' eventually amalgamated into the modern word kingfisher. The reverse, 'Fisher King', refers to an important character in the Arthurian Quest for the Holy Grail. Percival finds the Holy Grail in the castle of the Fisher King. This 1880s mural by August Spiess is in Neuschwanstein Castle, Bavaria.

temple of Userkaf at Saqqara (2490–2345 BCE) includes two lifeless species of kingfisher. Other tombs have marsh hunting scenes with a profusion of birds, some of which might be nebulous renderings of kingfishers. In the time of Tutankhamun, during the Amarna period (1332–1323 BCE), the static, highly stylized approach of Egyptians artists changed. Eternity was of less consequence than the current exciting adventure of living. In *The*

This 2500s BCE stone relief is from the mortuary temple of Userkaf at Saqqara, Egypt. The common kingfisher (*Alcedo atthis*) is perched on the far left and a pied kingfisher (*Ceryle rudis*) is hovering in the centre.

Culture of Ancient Egypt (1951), John Albert Wilson uses a superb wall painting of a pied kingfisher from the northern palace of Akhenaten to exemplify this change. Wilson describes the bird as 'caught at the very moment of its dive, the instant of arrested power before lightning-quick movement . . . [the] kingfisher in the fresco, seem to be tensed for immediate action because of an inner emotional excitement'.[25]

A different type of abundance is represented in many seventeenth-century Dutch still-life paintings. They too are about the bounty of nature combined with the success of the hunt. The inclusion of kingfishers in these canvases strongly suggests that they, and the rest of the birds depicted, are destined for the table. But not every table. It must be remembered that, as per Linnaeus' description (see Chapter One), kingfishers are in a group of birds that eat 'filthy substances'. In the same period, when 'after the hunt' still-life paintings were in vogue, Europeans were for the most part readers of the Old Testament, in which God instructs Moses and Aaron on which animals of the land, water and air can and cannot be eaten. A common denominator of unclean animals is that they are observed to kill and eat other animals. Non-kosher or unclean birds are listed in Leviticus 11:13–19, 42–3 and Deuteronomy 14:11–18. Kingfishers are not specifically mentioned in these two passages, but two other piscivores – cormorants and herons – are singled out as unclean. Like herons, kingfishers do not eat carrion directly but are consumers of animals such as bottom-feeding fish and crustaceans, as well as creatures that slither on the ground that eat detritus or carrion. A kingfisher's diet is loaded with unclean foods such as crustaceans, insects, frogs, salamanders, snakes and the occasional bottom-feeding fish. The possibility exists that kingfishers are included in the paintings as an artifice – an element of colour – but this is unlikely.

This John Gerrard Keulemans drawing of 1902, features two birds; the North Solomons dwarf kingfisher (*Ceyx meeki*) is almost a background element for the Borneo black-faced pitta.

During the era of the great voyages of discovery led by Captain Cook and others, the race was on to name all living and extinct flora and fauna. During these voyages, type specimens were collected and preserved. Freezers did not exist, of course, so getting rid of all body tissues that might rot or putrefy was essential, as

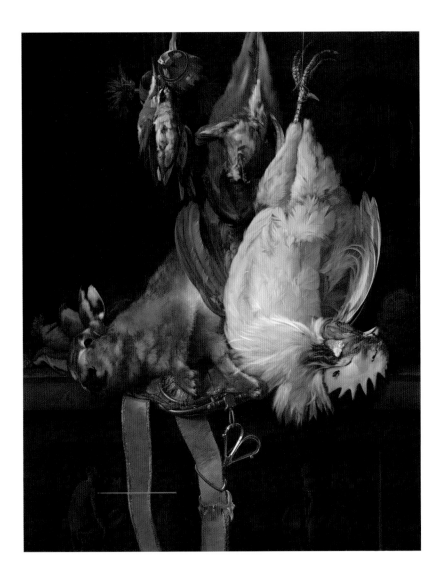

John Gerrard Keulemans illustrated Richard B. Sharpe's kingfisher monograph of 1871. This illustration of an African dwarf kingfisher (*Ispidina lecontie*) was based on museum skins and field notebooks, since neither the artist nor the author had ever seen one.

was protecting the resulting pelt, or bones, from insects, ship rats and anything else that might devour or blemish them. Arsenic soap was the preservative of choice. After a voyage ended, an alleged new species was compared with existing museum specimens and all known taxonomic literature to ascertain if it was indeed 'new'. The final step was the publishing of a book or article, thereby affixing a name to a hitherto unknown specimen. This first documentation of a species' existence had to discuss its kinship to other species, plus all of its defining characteristics. An illustration commonly augmented text descriptions. In the 1700s and 1800s, hand-tinted copperplate engravings were the norm.

Willem van Aelst's *Still-life with Dead Birds and Game Bag* (1674) is very typical of the genre. A common kingfisher (at the top, left of centre) is suspended with other game.

In the case of kingfishers, a plethora of scientific drawings exist, executed by some of the most famous names in ornithology – John Gerrard Keulemans, John Gould, John James Audubon, Louis Agassiz – plus a veritable host of other great artists. The skill of these individuals is such that the prints project an aura of calm, as if the viewer is actually there, in a distant land, observing the birds.

Audubon paintings were so popular that acknowledged 'fake' prints were produced. Robert Havell duplicated this hand-coloured etching and aquatint of a belted kingfisher in 1830.

Vincent van Gogh owned a common kingfisher (*Alcedo atthis*) skin. In 1887, Van Gogh used the skin as a model for his painting *Kingfisher by the Waterside*. Both the kingfisher skin and this painting are housed at the Van Gogh Museum.

In approximately 1870, the Victorian art critic John Ruskin painted this elegantly simple common kingfisher (*Alcedo atthis*). Ruskin's use of a white background accentuates how truly magnificent the plumage of this species is.

Many artists not associated with biology, biologists or taxonomic publications of any kind draw inspiration from museum specimens or produce works that are similar in nature to taxonomic prints. John Ruskin, Victorian author, art critic, defender of J.M.W. Turner and champion of the Pre-Raphaelites, executed his kingfisher painting in 1870–71. The white background coupled with the frozen appearance of his common kingfisher open up the possibility that a taxidermic mount was the model. Considering Ruskin's involvement with the Pre-Raphaelites, one would suspect that he would have been inclined towards painting *en plein air*.[26] Vincent van Gogh owned the taxidermy kingfisher depicted in his 1887 painting *Kingfisher by the Waterside*. After Van Gogh's death, his stuffed kingfisher was donated by the family to the Van Gogh Museum, Amsterdam, where it is occasionally displayed alongside the painting. When placed on a table, Van Gogh kingfisher's naturally rests in the same pose he painted, a most un-kingfisher-like position. Detailed studies of this painting have concluded that he painted the bird first and added the background and the feet later. The Van Gogh Museum's online catalogue states: 'Comparing this painting to the mounted bird, one notices a couple of differences. Van Gogh made the tail slightly longer in the painting, probably to achieve a balance with the raised beak.'[27]

Van Gogh, in keeping with other Art Nouveau, Impressionist and Post-Impressionist artists, was interested in *Japonisme*. He owned several prints of Japanese woodcuts, including Utagawa Hiroshige ii's *Arrowhead and Kingfisher*. In many Japanese

Japanese woodblock prints frequently include kingfishers. The above Utagawa Hiroshige ii print, called *Kingfisher and Reeds*, is from 1853.

woodcuts, the composition is set out on a single plane with the vantage point slightly above and from a slight angle. The composition and style of all four of Van Gogh's bird pictures – his kingfisher canvas plus two owl and one swift sketch – are experiments in *japonisme*.[28]

A few years earlier, in 1884, Van Gogh had created a large work which he called *The Kingfisher*. In this instance, he was inspired by Jules Breton's poem 'Automne'. Van Gogh sent this pencil, ink and gouache drawing to the artist Anthon van Rappard and shortly thereafter sent Van Rappard a copy of the poem on which the scene was based. In this atmospheric composition, the title is key to noticing that there is a tiny kingfisher hovering in the centre.[29]

Recently, a kingfisher was discovered in a most unlikely place. Beneath the grease and grim of centuries, two brushstrokes emerged almost centre stage in John Constable's painting *The Mill Stream*. In 1814, Constable applied a bright blue dab of paint slightly above a red one to simulate a common kingfisher traversing the pond.

Kingfisher depictions in popular art range from realistic to playful, serene to menacing, all-seeing watchmen. Fairytales feature kingfishers as decorative elements and occasionally as important cast members. In a reworking of Richard Johnson's 1621 poem 'The History of Tom Thumbe', the 1957 edition of *Playhour Annual* substituted a common kingfisher for a raven as the bird that swoops down, snatches Tom in its talons and transports him to the castle of the giant. Tom being no taller than his father's thumb makes this feat feasible.[30]

Utterly playful and featured in several cartoons is the song with the opening line: 'Kookaburra up in the old gum tree'. The song was written in 1932 by the Australian music teacher Marion Sinclair. In 1934 'Kookaburra' won the Girl Guides Association of Victoria song competition. That year, in front of Lord and Lady

Baden-Powell, it was performed for the first time at an Australian jamboree. Over the decades, multiple variations of the lyrics have evolved, but invariably the phrase 'Laugh kookaburra, laugh' remains intact.

The influence and appearance of kingfishers in Western writing and art go back for centuries. At the non-literary end of the spectrum, kingfishers have played their part in prodding intellectuals to develop new theories or lines of inquiry. In today's visual culture, kingfishers are less mystical, less tied to tradition,

This 1874 *Picture Alphabet of Birds* came with rhyming text. The quatrain for the kingfisher reads: 'Upon the streamlet's reedy bank / The quick Kingfisher see; / Soon, soon within his long sharp bill / A quiv'ring fish will be.'

The British folkloric figure Tom Thumb has been at the heart of many publications over the centuries. This playful illustration accompanied the 1957 *Playhour Annual* rendition of this classic tale. In it a kingfisher, rather than a raven, swoops up and transports Tom to the castle of a giant.

and less inclined to be the muses of intellectuals and scientists. The majority of iconic kingfishers depicted in the next chapter have roles akin to the bird in the 'Kookaburra' song. Their depictions are uplifting, a connection with nature and occasionally comical.

6 Iconic Kingfishers

Kingfisher branding is everywhere, whether on hotels, motels, restaurants and businesses that are actually called 'kingfisher something' or as the emblem of establishments and businesses with totally unrelated names. The link between something named 'kingfisher' and what it actually is need not be obvious. The thoroughbred stallion Kingfisher made horse-racing history in 1870 when he won the Belmont Stakes, the longest and most gruelling of the American Triple Crown races, going on to earn a significant sum of money from stud fees. Mochrum Kingfisher, a champion Belted Galloway bull, is very much alive and is earning a good income siring a dynasty.

The use of kingfisher logos and mascots to promote nature is a worldwide phenomenon. A white-throated kingfisher is the logo of Keoladeo National Park, a UNESCO World Heritage Site in eastern Rajasthan, India. This man-made wetland sanctuary was originally created to protect the region from flooding, provide grazing for village cattle and (in the past) provide waterfowl hunting grounds for maharajahs. Out of the approximately four hundred resident birds, plus all the flora and other animals that call these ponds and marshlands home, the white-throated kingfisher won the mascot lottery.

The national bird of the Republic of Cabo Verde (Cape Verde Islands) is a grey-headed kingfisher. Great Britain held an online vote to select a national bird in 2015. The common kingfisher was on the ballot but ended a distant sixth to the easier-to-find, more inquisitive European robin.

Kingfishers are used in heraldry. Several regions include them on their crests and flags. The Australian City of Maroondah, Bowral and Blacktown City all feature one or more laughing kookaburras on their coats of arms. From 1982 until 1988, the Malaysian State of Sabah had a crest dominated by a sacred kingfisher. For the Malaysia-resident Sama-Bajau people, kingfishers are messengers of the gods. Halifax Regional Municipality, the capital of the Canadian province of Nova Scotia, has a blue silhouette of a belted kingfisher in the very centre of its flag and coat of arms. One of the former flags of the city of Halifax featured only a kingfisher, an often-used heraldic symbol of the fishing industry.

The 2000 Summer Olympics in Sydney, Australia featured three official mascots representing air, soil and water. Olly (Olympics), a laughing kookaburra, exemplified the Olympic spirit of generosity; Millie (Millennium), an echidna with the abilities of a numerical guru, represented technology; and Syd (City of Sydney), a platypus, embodied the environment as well as activity and energy. During the games, this larger-than-life trio got up to all sorts of mischief.

Britain's Wildfowl and Wetlands Trust (WWT), a conservation charity, has a collection of giant Lego wetland animals that tours its nine UK wetland centres. Since their debut in 2015, Kate the Kingfisher and her Lego friends have greeted many visitors among their real-life cousins. Nick Brooks, General Manager of WWT Martin Mere Wetland Centre, has said, 'Our visitors, young and old, absolutely love our giant Lego brick animals and Kate the Kingfisher is a particular favourite. They are all a really fun way to highlight some of the animals WWT helps to protect, such as the kingfisher, the iconic Nene and our otters. We are using Lego bricks

The coat of arms of the City of Blacktown embraces an Aboriginal head, a wattle and a boomerang. The shield is supported by a horse and a kangaroo. The kookaburra at the top is holding a boomerang in its foot.

The common kingfishers (*Alcedo atthis*) of the Notte Canal are the inspiration for the coat of arms of Kallinchen, a small village south of Berlin, Germany.

Ringwood, now part of the City of Maroondah (a suburb of Melbourne, Australia) opted to replace the blackbirds on the English city crest of the same name with kookaburras – a tradition that has been incorporated into the City of Maroondah crest.

to inspire the next generation to continue our work of saving threatened wetland wildlife.'[1] Often running at the same time are interactive Lego workshops, creating an opportunity for budding sculptors to build their own Kate the Kingfisher mini-figurines. Several Lego kingfisher kits exist. Blake the blue-winged kooka-burra is part of the 2013 Oceania Series. Amber the azure kingfisher comes complete with prey; five grey fish dangle from her beak. Kingsley the kingfisher, an especially clever design by Thomas Poulsom, has two modes: wings demurely closed or flamboyantly outstretched. The latter is achieved by inserting additional Lego bricks to create blue, white and turquoise fan-like wings. The MOCpages website, a fan site not affiliated with Lego, has pages listing biological and ecological facts for many of these figurines.

Globally, the best-known kingfisher logo is a beer brand. King-fisher beer signs are prominent on the Indian subcontinent. Based in the southern state of Karnataka, the parent company opened its doors as Castle Breweries in 1957. Subsequently, Castle Brew-eries amalgamated with four of its competitors to become United Breweries. In the 1970s the company went international, launching the Kingfisher brand in 1978. Flying above a red banner embla-zoned with 'KINGFISHER' in bold white letters is the bird itself. India is home to a dozen kingfisher species. The company website is silent on why the common kingfisher was chosen. Perhaps using the most cosmopolitan of kingfishers in the act of flying was a subliminal message of the company's international expan-sion goals, plus common kingfishers would be more familiar, more instantly recognizable, to most Europeans. Perhaps someone in the company liked kingfishers and there is no deep underlying meaning.

Holding a 50 per cent share, United Breweries Group founded Kingfisher Airlines Limited. Branded as 'Kingfisher Red', this low-cost Indian airline based out of Mumbai went bankrupt in 2013, less than eight years after its maiden flight. United Breweries had better luck when they partnered with the East Bengal Football Club. The newly minted Kingfisher East Bengal FC retained the club's original logo, adding the beer brand's thick red border with the word 'Kingfisher' embedded in it.[2]

Walmart has a humble connection with kingfishers. 'Mr Sam', as the founder Samuel Walton is known, was born in the town of Kingfisher, Oklahoma. Walmart has never elected to incorporate a kingfisher into its logo, even though it has a better claim than some. Woolworths Holdings (owner of B&Q, Superdrug and Comet) rebranded itself as Kingfisher plc in 1989. Based in Paddington, Kingfisher plc is traded on the London stock exchange as KGF. It is the largest home-improvement retailer in Europe

The United Breweries Group 'Kingfisher' brand has several marketing campaigns. The label on the left is targeted at the sports market (specifically cricket); the label on the left is an upscale version of their classic label.

This belted kingfisher (*Megacerycle alcyon*) card from the *Birds of America* series was issued by Allen & Ginter to promote their cigarette brand in 1888. By lithographing these 'stiffener cards', this company created the hobby of card collecting.

and the third-largest in the world. The logo of this multinational company appears mid-word as an extremely stylized common kingfisher created by two paintbrush strokes suggesting the letter 'F' and the bird at the same time.

The stylized, familiar logo of automobile manufacturer Subaru has a tenuous kingfisher connection. The Japanese name for the closest star cluster to Earth is Subaru. In English, these stars are known as the Pleiades or, alternatively, the Seven Sisters; each one is named after one of the seven daughters of Atlas and Pleione, with the brightest and biggest being Alcyone. The heroine of *Wish Upon the Pleiades*, a 2011 anime produced by Gainax with Subaru, is Subaru, a pink-haired schoolgirl whose passion is astronomy. Not unlike Alcyone, Subaru shares a strong sense of purpose and can inhabit two forms. Alcyone is both a dutiful wife and a kingfisher; Subaru is both a clumsy schoolgirl and a magical girl with super-powers.

Allen & Ginter, a brand of hand-rolled cigarettes formally based out of Richmond, Virginia, is best remembered for its invention of collectible trading cards. Soft cigarette packages of the 1880s had a stiff paper card enclosed to protect the cigarettes. When Allen & Ginter began production in 1865, this structural stiffener was blank. In 1886, the company opted to advertise their brand via lithographs printed on these package stiffeners. The craze for these colourful cards reached Europe in 1888, when W. D. & H. O. Wills, a British cigarette manufacturer, followed suit. Allen & Ginter and other cigarette companies launched many series over the years. Covering an encyclopaedic range of topics from war to nature, the company is best remembered for their sports cards. Kingfishers featured in two Allen & Ginter collector series: a belted kingfisher is part of the Birds of North America (1888) series, while a sacred kingfisher is part of the Birds of the Tropics (1889) set. In a 1922 Do You Know series, Wills's cigarettes featured a 'A Laughing Jackass'. The reverse side of these collector cards listed facts, in this instance habitat and food preferences of laughing kookaburras.

The cigarette company John Player & Sons used a similar template when they produced collector card No. 22 in their 1939 'British Naval Craft' series depicting HMS *Halcyon*. The reverse tells us that the *Halcyon* was 'the prototype of a class of seventeen minesweepers built during 1933–1938'. HMS *Halcyon* was named perhaps with the hope that it would only encounter calm seas. The Halcyon class served during the Second World War in home waters and in the Mediterranean, and did convoy duty in the Atlantic and Arctic in their capacity as minesweepers and anti-submarine escorts. During the evacuation of Dunkirk, the Halcyon class of ships is estimated to have rescued 14,000 people.[3]

Vought OS2U Kingfisher aircraft have no similarities to their living namesake other than having a single set of wings. Single-pontoon planes, they were fabricated in Philadelphia, Pennsylvania, commencing in 1938. Designed and built for the U.S. Navy, these catapult-launched monoplane observation aircraft were used extensively in the Second World War by the Americans, as well as by the British Royal Navy and the Royal Australian Air Force. Before the days of radar, the pilot flying a Kingfisher provided an essential service. Gunners on ships firing on targets out of visual range needed to be told their co-ordinates. Kingfisher pilots not only sent target information to the gunners but also reported back on the accuracy of their fire. As 'scouts', Vought OS2U Kingfisher planes functioned as ships' eyes, locating enemy surface ships and submarines and thus warding off surprise attacks and enabling defensive action. These compact mid-wing monoplanes, typically equipped with one large central pontoon and a small stabilizing pontoon attached to each wing, are extremely odd-looking. All the noble and regal kingfisher

This catapult-launched Vought os2u Kingfisher is a compact mid-wing monoplane, equipped with one large central pontoon and two small stabilizing pontoons. One plane enthusiast placed this odd-looking plane on his 'ugly-duckling list'.

descriptors fall by the wayside when describing a Vought os2u aircraft, but they were reliable and very successful at executing the tasks for which they were designed. One plane enthusiast placed them on his 'ugly-duckling list'.[4]

The letters of the Lockheed AQM-60 Kingfisher stand for (A) air, (Q) drone and (M) guided missile. These 11.6-metre missiles with a 3-metre wingspan were utilized to test anti-missile systems in the 1950s by simulating incoming enemy planes or missiles. They proved to be too good. These drones evaded the hypersonic anti-missile weapons systems designed to destroy them and opened up the question of the overall effectiveness of the u.s. Air Force's anti-missile systems, much to the embarrassment of the system's designers and to the glee of the Kingfisher missile engineers.

158

There is no common thread uniting the above random jumble of products, companies and places that are called 'kingfisher something' or that have a kingfisher mascot. It is not always intuitive why the word *kingfisher* or the image of one has been called into play. Whether the universal appeal of kingfishers is due to interactions some of us have with these feathered fiends or because we subconsciously imbue them with human attributes such as reliability, success or exemplary moral behaviour is academic. Advertisers capitalize on our yearnings for connection with the natural world. Often starting with a most unnatural product, they seek to normalize it; linking it visually, or in our imaginations, with an exemplary icon of flora or fauna is common practice. Our minds are diverted to the exquisite form, or the delightful colouration, or the implied abilities or prowess of this paragon of strength or virtue. How 'kingfishers catch fire' and how a 'kingfisher jewelling upstream seems to leave a streak of

The 11.6-metre-long Lockheed Kingfisher supersonic guided target missiles were specifically designed to test anti-missile systems in the 1950s as a proxy for incoming enemy planes (or missiles).

Issued in 2017, this Australian one-ounce silver coin has two laughing kookaburras (*Dacelo novaeguineae*) on the reverse side.

itself in the bright air' is part of our collective memory.[5] In the hands of an advertising design team, kingfishers, with their striking silhouettes, dazzling colours and mutability, make themselves ideal branding candidates. Be it beer or battleships, the very thought of kingfishers makes us feel good. These mesmerizing birds are part of our nature heritage. For millennia they have been part of our cultural heritage, and they continue to be reinvented and incorporated into popular culture today.

7 Masters of Two Mediums

Biomimicry is a design and engineering approach that turns to nature to find solutions. Rather than reinvent the wheel, researchers look for a plant, an invertebrate or an animal that has solved the problem under investigation. Other ways of referring to biomicry are: What would nature do? Or, put more simply: Ask nature. Designers look at 3.8 billion years of evolution to solve engineering problems. Little wonder that biomimicry engineers and scientists find how kingfishers enter water intriguing.

Kingfishers are famed for their diving skills. Their long, dagger-shaped beaks cleave the water's surface, scarcely creating a ripple. The bodies of kingfishers enter the water by either compressing the wings distally or by arching the wings over thew back. These diving strategies elongate the head and neck, thus delaying the inevitable splash when both wings and body penetrate the air/water interface.

In cross-section, each half of a common kingfisher's beak is triangular with curved sides. Joined together, as they are when the bird dives, the beak shape resembles a squashed diamond.[1] It is this 'perfect' shape that enables a River Kingfisher's beak to penetrate water, seamlessly exiting the aerial world into the denser aquatic realm. Fish are not defenceless, however. Running down both their sides are lateral sense organs capable of detecting minute vibrations, movements or pressure gradient differences in the surrounding water. Being the masters of two mediums, kingfishers have perfected the art of penetrating water by barely disturbing the environment surrounding a fish in order to catch it unawares.

The beak morphology of common kingfishers was used to resolve difficulties concerning the Japanese 300 series Shinkansen high-speed 'bullet train'. When exiting tunnels, the train would create mini-explosions. These explosions were not as deafening as the sonic boom fighter jets produce when breaking the sound barrier, but they were similar. The resulting noise pollution within a 400-metre radius of some tunnel exits was unacceptable. The problem was the tunnel's hard interior surfaces, acting as a cylinder impeding air from escaping in all directions. Piston-like, a train speeding through a tunnel pushes air ahead of itself, creating pressure waves. Depending on the length and topography of the tunnel, these pressure waves sometimes gain speeds approaching that of sound. When these low-frequency air waves escaped the confines of the tunnels, they produced an audible popping, booming or high-decibel sound as the trains emerged. Engineer Eiji Nakatsu and his team solved this noise-pollution problem by studying what they considered to be the most efficient creature to transition through two mediums – the common kingfisher. Their biomimicry studies of how kingfishers transition from a low-pressure environment (air) to a high-pressure one (water) resulted in a revolutionary locomotive nose-cone design. To test their theories, they created bullets of various shapes and fired them through a pipe. Actual measurements from these experiments plus computer simulations mimicked trains speeding through tunnels. 'Data analysis showed that the ideal shape for the Shinkansen is almost identical to a kingfisher's beak,' explained Nakatsu in an interview.[2] The reconfigured 500 series Shinkansen trains used 15 per cent less electricity. This kingfisher-inspired nose-cone design increased train speeds by 10 per cent while reducing pressure waves created in tunnels by 30 per cent, thus greatly reducing or even eliminating the sonic-boom problems.[3] Another welcome by-product of the design was a more comfortable ride. Formerly, train interiors felt smaller when travelling through tunnels due to a sudden change in air resistance. Hard as it is to fathom, the fact that common kingfishers have perfected a flawless, nearly 'splash-less' dive over the millennia is daily helping tens of thousands of commuters to get home comfortably in time for dinner.

The ongoing invention of high-tech measuring instruments is opening up a treasure trove of opportunities for the study of bio-mimicry. Exploring why the common kingfisher is the master of two mediums has not only had positive results for Japanese commuters but has irreversibly altered locomotive design concepts globally. If and when the expert hovering skills of pied kingfishers come under the bio-engineering lens, insights gained from yet another kingfisher species might lead once again to revolutionary designs concepts that help commuters.

The common kingfishers of Great Britain and Japan are one and the same. *Alcedo atthis* inhabits the largest geographic range of any kingfisher species. This lively sprite living in so many regions of Eurasia has evolved different mythologies, symbolism, and literary references in a myriad of languages and cultures. Observations of the habits, hunting skills, breeding systems, calls and outward appearance of the plethora of kingfisher species are reflected in their different mythical personalities recorded in legends, teaching stories, literature and iconography.

Based on the European experience, this bird family is internationally known as the kingfisher family. This appellation is an oxymoron for most of the Alcedinidae, since only one in five

A common kingfisher (*Alcedo atthis*) preparing to make a clean entry into water.

actually has piscatorial tendencies. If the name 'icebird' had prevailed, that would have been even less appropriate. If Linnaeus had been aware of pied kingfisher trios, controlling kookaburra mothers and the murderous intent of some kookaburra siblings, would 'The Myth of the Halcyon' have come to mind when he was mulling over what to name this charismatic family of Coraciiformes? The myths in Ovid's poems include multiple deities and mortals participating in siblicide, trios and marital infidelity, giving Linnaeus a host of personages to draw upon if he had wanted to invoke the sinister side of some members of the kingfisher family. But the finer details of some of these radical southern-hemisphere fringe members of the kingfisher clan would not be discovered for another two hundred years.

Over the centuries, kingfishers have provoked much thought as well as serving as artistic and literary muses. Now, with the advent of biomimicry research, they have become design and engineering muses too.

No other species of kingfisher comes close to having the flying skills of the pied kingfisher (*Ceryle rudis*). Not only do they fly long distances from shore, but their aerial dance is reminiscent of the hovering skills of hummingbirds. They are the only kingfisher able to eat on the wing.

Andy Morffew's masterly image captures this common kingfisher erupting out of water with its prey. These superb avian fishers are equally spectacular in all elements of the chase: the dive, the underwater pursuit and exiting the water.

Timeline of the Kingfisher

c. 66 MYA

Four bird lineages survive the K-Pg extinction

c. 47.8 33.9 MYA

The fossil *Quasisyndactylus longibrachis* (Mayr, 1998) is the ancestor of all living kingfishers

c. 27.1 MYA

Crown group of kingfishers evolves in Indomalayan realm

c. 25 MYA

Subfamilies of Water Kingfishers (Cerylinae) and Tree Kingfishers (Daceloninae) diverge from each other

---

c. 1.8 MYA

Halcyon (a Tree Kingfisher) colonize Africa. Later, they recolonize Asia

1332–1323 BCE

Egyptian mortuary art often includes kingfishers in marsh hunting scenes

c. 300 BCE

In *History of Animals*, Aristotle incorrectly states that kingfishers nest in sea balls. First record of the existence of *tian-tsui* objects, a Chinese art form similar to cloisonné that utilizes kingfisher feathers

8 BCE

Ovid finishes his *Metamorphoses*, which includes his epic poem 'The Myth of the Halcyon'.

802–1431 CE

The Khmer Empire (Cambodia) exports dead and living kingfishers to China. This lucrative commodity helps fund the building of Angkor Wat

---

1871

Richard B. Sharpe, then librarian of the Zoological Society of London, authors the first kingfisher monograph

1888

Allen & Ginter print promotional material on the stiffening cards inside their cigarette packages, inadvertently starting the collector card hobby

1908

Empress Dowager Cixi of China dies. The last Chinese emperor abdicates four years later, ending the need for *tian-tsui* (kingfisher feather) court regalia

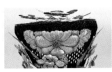

c. 16.3 MYA	*c.* 8 MYA	*c.* 7.7 MYA	*c.* 1.9 MYA
Modern genera of Cerylinae and Daceloninae begin colonizing Australia	*Chloroceryle* kingfishers colonize the Americas	River Kingfishers (Alcedininae) cvolve in Wallacea	*Megaceryle* (a Water Kingfisher) colonize the Americas. Later, they recolonize Africa and Asia

1567	1758	1832
Arthur Golding's English translation of Ovid's *Metamorphoses* is published. It becomes a reference book for Shakespeare and others	Drawing inspiration from Ovid's 'Myth of the Halcyon', Linnaeus formulates scientific names for kingfishers that he publishes in the tenth edition of *Systema Naturae*	Charles Darwin's very first bird notation while on HMS *Beagle* is about a kingfisher

1953	1978	1996	2015
Charles Olson writes his poem 'The Kingfisher', utilizing his projective verse theory	United Brewers introduce their Kingfisher beer. Their affiliate, Kingfisher Airlines, files for bankruptcy in 2012 after only eight years in operation	Biomimicry engineering techniques based on common kingfisher beaks is used to redesign Japan's high-speed 500 Series Shinkansen locomotives	Kate the Kingfisher, and several other giant Lego sculptures, begin touring British Wildfowl & Wetlands Trust (WWT) centres.

Appendix 1
Global List of Kingfishers

Choosing which of the four recognized avian taxonomic lists to follow is not a simple task. Each has its own committee of well-respected and globally recognized experts. The top four global avian taxonomic lists are:

The Clements Checklist of the Birds of the World, 2017
Handbook of Birds of the World Alive
The Howard and Moore Complete Checklist of the Birds of the World, 4th edn
IOC World Bird List, version 7.3

All these lists have their strong points. Every species on these lists has undergone a review process, but the outcome is not always the same. The number of recognized kingfisher species varies from 114 to 120. The number of accepted species is sure to increase as currently proposed species splits and amalgamations are verified and incorporated into these lists. Currently, kingfisher phylogenics is an active and dynamic research topic. It is going to take a decade or more to complete systematic research on all the kingfisher genera and species complexes. When this work is completed, the avian taxonomic community may or may not, reach a consensus on exactly how many kingfisher species exist.

I have elected to use the most conservative list, the IOC World Bird List (version 7.3), edited by Frank Gill and David Donsker, as a baseline for taxonomic and English kingfisher names. This version of the list, which recognizes 114 kingfisher species, is available in various formats and languages at www.worldbirdnames.org/ioc-lists/master-list-2.

Capitalization and hyphenation are not consistent in the lists cited above. In this book, I am using a blend of styles, for example:

Hombron's [blue-capped] kingfisher, *Actenoides hombroni* (vu)
dimorphic dwarf kingfisher, *Ceyx margarethae* (lc)

In the first example, the first word is the ioc common name. In square brackets is an alternate name assigned to this species by one or more of the other widely accepted taxonomic naming systems.

I have elected to put the colloquial subfamily name first with the taxonomic subfamily name in brackets. The order in which the sub-families should be listed varies. In this appendix, the order is: River–Water–Tree, equivalent to Alcedinae–Cerylinae–Daceloninae.

A detailed discussion of kingfisher sub-species is beyond the scope of this book. When a sub-species is a key component of a story, they are included. A subspecies can be recognized by their trinomial name or when the species name has been abbreviated to one letter. For example, the Bougainville moustached kingfisher is *Actenoides bougainvillei bougainvillei* or *Actenoides b. bougainvillei*. Some subspecies have unique common names in English, but this is not always the case.

To give an indication of global status, each kingfisher species name is followed by its iucn (International Union for the Conservation of Nature) Red List two-letter code in brackets (accessed 15 November 2017). (For range maps and additional information, please go to the following website: http://datazone.birdlife.org/quicksearch?qs=kingfisher.)

The iucn Red List two-letter codes are as follows:

ex = Extinct
ew = Extinct in the Wild
cr = Critically Endangered
en = Endangered
vu = Vulnerable

NT = Near Threatened
LC = Least Concern
DD = Data Deficient

RIVER KINGFISHERS, *subfamily Alcedinae*

African pygmy kingfisher, *Ispidina picta* (LC)
African dwarf kingfisher, *Ispidina lecontei* (LC)
Madagascan [Madagascar] pygmy kingfisher, *Corythornis madagascariensis* (LC)
white bellied kingfisher, *Corythornis leucogaster* (LC)
malachite kingfisher, *Corythornis cristatus* (LC)
Malagasy [Madagascar] kingfisher, *Corythornis vintsioides* (LC)
cerulean kingfisher, *Alcedo coerulescens* (LC)
blue-banded kingfisher, *Alcedo euryzona* [*A. e. euryzona* (CR)]
shining-blue kingfisher, *Alcedo quadribrachys* (LC)
blue-eared kingfisher, *Alcedo meninting* (LC)
common kingfisher, *Alcedo atthis* (LC)
half-collared kingfisher, *Alcedo semitorquata* (LC)
Blyth's kingfisher, *Alcedo hercules* (NT)
Oriental dwarf kingfisher, *Ceyx erithaca* (LC)
Philippine dwarf kingfisher, *Ceyx melanurus* (VU)
Sulawesi dwarf kingfisher, C*eyx fallax* [*C. f. sangirensis* (CR)]
Moluccan dwarf kingfisher, *Ceyx lepidus* (LC)
dimorphic dwarf kingfisher, *Ceyx margarethae* (LC)
Sula dwarf kingfisher, *Ceyx wallacii* (NT)
Buru dwarf kingfisher, *Ceyx cajeli* (NT)
Papuan [New Guinea] dwarf kingfisher, *Ceyx solitarius* (LC)
Manus dwarf kingfisher, *Ceyx dispar* (NT)
New Ireland dwarf kingfisher, *Ceyx mulcatus* (LC)
New Britain dwarf kingfisher, *Ceyx sacerdotis* (LC)
North Solomons dwarf kingfisher, *Ceyx meeki* (LC)
New Georgia dwarf kingfisher, *Ceyx collectoris* (LC)
Malaita dwarf kingfisher, *Ceyx malaitae* (not yet assessed)
Guadalcanal dwarf kingfisher, *Ceyx nigromaxilla* (LC)

indigo-banded kingfisher, *Ceyx cyanopectus* (NT)
southern silvery kingfisher, *Ceyx argentatus* (NT)
northern silvery kingfisher, *Ceyx flumenicola* (NT)
azure kingfisher, *Ceyx azureus* (LC)
Bismarck kingfisher, *Ceyx websteri* (VU)
little kingfisher, *Ceyx pusillus* (LC)

WATER KINGFISHERS, *subfamily Cerylinae*

American pygmy kingfisher, *Chloroceryle aenea* (LC)
green-and-rufous kingfisher, *Chloroceryle inda* (LC)
green kingfisher, *Chloroceryle americana* (LC)
Amazon kingfisher, *Chloroceryle amazona* (LC)
crested kingfisher, *Megaceryle lugubris* (LC)
giant kingfisher, *Megaceryle maxima* (LC)
ringed kingfisher, *Megaceryle torquata* (LC)
belted kingfisher, *Megaceryle alcyon* (LC)
pied kingfisher, *Ceryle rudis* (LC)

TREE KINGFISHERS, *subfamily Daceloninae [formerly Halcyoninae]*

green-backed [blue-headed] kingfisher, *Actenoides monachus* (NT)
scaly-breasted kingfisher, *Actenoides princeps* (NT)
Bougainville moustached kingfisher, *Actenoides bougainvillei* (EN)
spotted kingfisher, *Actenoides lindsayi* (LC)
Hombron's [blue-capped] kingfisher, *Actenoides hombroni* (VU)
rufous-collared kingfisher, *Actenoides concretus* (NT)
hook-billed kingfisher, *Melidora macrorrhina* (LC)
banded kingfisher, *Lacedo pulchella* (LC)
common paradise kingfisher, *Tanysiptera galatea* (LC)
Kofiau paradise kingfisher, *Tanysiptera ellioti* (VU)
Biak paradise kingfisher, *Tanysiptera riedelii* (NT)
Numfor paradise kingfisher, *Tanysiptera carolinae* (NT)
little paradise kingfisher, *Tanysiptera hydrocharis* (DD)
buff-breasted paradise kingfisher, *Tanysiptera sylvia* (LC)

black-headed paradise kingfisher, *Tanysiptera nigriceps* (LC)
red-breasted paradise kingfisher, *Tanysiptera nympha* (LC)
brown-headed paradise kingfisher, *Tanysiptera danae* (LC)
lilac [Sulawesi lilac] kingfisher, C*ittura cyanotis* (LC)
shovel-billed kingfisher, C*lytoceyx rex* (LC)
laughing kookaburra, *Dacelo novaeguineae* (LC)
blue-winged kookaburra, *Dacelo leachii* (LC)
spangled kookaburra, *Dacelo tyro* (LC)
rufous-bellied kookaburra, *Dacelo gaudichaud* (LC)
glittering [white-rumped] kingfisher, C*aridonax fulgidus* (LC)
stork-billed kingfisher, *Pelargopsis capensis* (LC)
great-billed [black-billed] kingfisher, *Pelargopsis melanorhyncha* (LC)
brown-winged kingfisher, *Pelargopsis amauroptera* (NT)
ruddy kingfisher, *Halcyon coromanda* (LC)
white-throated [white-breasted] kingfisher, *Halcyon smyrnensis* (LC)
Javan kingfisher, *Halcyon cyanoventris* (LC)
chocolate-backed kingfisher, *Halcyon badia* (LC)
black-capped kingfisher, *Halcyon pileata* (LC)
grey-headed kingfisher, *Halcyon leucocephala* (LC)
brown-hooded kingfisher, *Halcyon albiventris* (LC)
striped kingfisher, *Halcyon chelicuti* (LC)
blue-breasted kingfisher, *Halcyon malimbica* (LC)
woodland kingfisher, *Halcyon senegalensis* (LC)
mangrove kingfisher, *Halcyon senegaloides* (LC)
blue-black kingfisher, *Todiramphus nigrocyaneus* (DD)
Winchell's [rufous-lored] kingfisher, *Todiramphus winchelli* (VU)
blue-and-white kingfisher, *Todiramphus diops* (LC)
lazuli kingfisher, *Todiramphus lazuli* (NT)
forest kingfisher, *Todiramphus macleayii* (LC)
white-mantled [New Britain] kingfisher, *Todiramphus albonotatus* (NT)
ultramarine kingfisher, *Todiramphus leucopygius* (LC)
Vanuatu kingfisher, *Todiramphus farquhari* (NT)
sombre kingfisher, *Todiramphus funebris* (VU)
collared kingfisher, *Todiramphus chloris* (LC)
Torresian kingfisher, *Todiramphus sordidus* (not yet assessed)

islet kingfisher, *Todiramphus colonus* (not yet assessed)
Melanesian kingfisher, *Todiramphus tristrami* (not yet assessed)
Pacific kingfisher, *Todiramphus sacer* (not yet assessed)
Talaud kingfisher, *Todiramphus enigma* (NT)
collared kingfisher, *Todiramphus chloris* (LC)
Guam kingfisher, *Todiramphus cinnamominus* (EW)
rusty-capped [Palau] kingfisher, *Todiramphus pelewensis* (NT)
Pohnpei kingfisher, *Todiramphus reichenbachii* (VU)
beach kingfisher *Todiramphus saurophagus* (LC)
sacred kingfisher, *Todiramphus sanctus* (LC)
flat-billed kingfisher, *Todiramphus recurvirostris* (LC)
cinnamon-banded kingfisher, *Todiramphus australasia* (NT)
chattering kingfisher, *Todiramphus tutus* (LC)
mewing [Mangaia] kingfisher, *Todiramphus ruficollaris* (VU)
chattering kingfisher, *Todiramphus tutus* (LC)
Society kingfisher, *Todiramphus venerates* (NT)
Mangareva [Tuamotu] kingfisher, *Todiramphus gambieri* (CR)
Niau kingfisher, *Todiramphus gertrudaci* (not yet assessed)
Marquesas kingfisher, *Todiramphus godeffroyi* (CR)
red-backed kingfisher, *Todiramphus pyrrhopygius* (LC)
yellow-billed kingfisher, *Syma torotoro* (LC)
mountain kingfisher, *Syma megarhyncha* (LC)

Appendix II
Kingfisher Species in Trouble

Birdlife International is the official International Union for the Conservation of Nature (IUCN) Red List authority for birds. This informative website lists the global status of all kingfisher species: http://datazone.birdlife.org/quicksearch?qs=kingfisher, accessed 15 November 2017.

EW = EXTINCT IN THE WILD

Guam kingfisher, *Todiramphus cinnamominus* (EW)

CE = CRITICALLY ENDANGERED

Sangihe dwarf kingfisher, *Ceyx sangirensis* (CR)
Javan blue-banded kingfisher, *Alcedo e. euryzona* (CR)
Tuamotu kingfisher, *Todiramphus gambieri* (CR)
Marquesas kingfisher, *Todiramphus godeffroyi* (CR)

EN = ENDANGERED

Bougainville moustached kingfisher, *Actenoides b. bougainvillei* (EN)
Guadalcanal moustached kingfisher, *Actenoides b. excelsus* (EN)
(Depending on the source, the two species above are either one or two species.)

North Philippine dwarf kingfisher, *Ceyx melanurus* (VU)
South Philippine dwarf kingfisher, *Ceyx mindanensis* (VU)
(Depending on the source, the two species above are either one or two species.)
plain-backed kingfisher, *Actenoides regalis* (VU)
Bismarck kingfisher, *Ceyx websteri* (VU)
blue-capped kingfisher, *Actenoides hombroni* (VU)
rufous-lored kingfisher, *Todiramphus winchelli* (VU)
sombre kingfisher, *Todiramphus funebris* (VU)
Mangaia kingfisher, *Todiramphus ruficollaris* (VU)
Pohnpei kingfisher, *Todiramphus reichenbachii* (VU)
Kofiau paradise kingfisher, *Tanysiptera ellioti* (VU)

DD = DATA DEFICIENT

There is not enough known, insufficient observations and/or data available to give these two species a rating.

blue-black kingfisher, *Todiramphus nigrocyaneus* (DD)
little paradise kingfisher, *Tanysiptera hydrocharis* (DD)

References

INTRODUCTION: A REALM OF KINGFISHERS

1 Caroli Linnaei, *Systema Naturae*, 10th edn (Stockholm, 1758).
2 Jonathan Bate, 'Shakespeare's Ovid', in *Ovid's Metamorphoses: The Arthur Golding Translation* [1567], ed. John Frederick Nims (Philadelphia, PA, 2000), p. XIII.
3 'Glossary of Collective Nouns by Subject', https://en.wiktionary. org, accessed 2 January 2017.

1 FOSSIL BRETHREN AND LIVING KIN

1 'Raptor Facts', http://raptorrehab.cvm.missouri.edu, accessed 26 July 2017.
2 Carl von Linné, *A General System of Nature: Through the Three Grand Kingdoms of Animals, Vegetables, and Minerals, Systematically Divided into Several Classes, Orders, Genera, Species, and Varieties*, trans. William Turton (London, 1802), vol. I, p. 132.
3 Gary W. Kaiser, *The Inner Bird: Anatomy and Evolution* (Vancouver, 2007), p. 244.
4 Richard O. Prum et al., 'A Comprehensive Phylogeny of Birds (Aves) Using Targeted Next-generation DNA Sequencing', *Nature*, DXXVI (2015), pp. 569–73.
5 Ivan R. Schwab and Nathan S. Hart, 'Halcyon Days', *Journal of Ophthalmology*, LXXXVIII (2008), p. 613.
6 Ivan R. Schwab, *Evolutions Witness: How Eyes Evolved* (New York, 2012), p. 195.
7 Ibid., p. 192.

8 Kevin Caley, 'Fossil Birds', in *Handbook of the Birds of the World*, ed. Josep del Hoyo, Andrew Elliott and David A. Christie (Barcelona, 2007), vol. XII, p. 11.

9 Robert G. Moyle, 'A Molecular Phylogeny of Kingfishers (Alcedinidae) with Insights into Early Biogeographic History', *The Auk*, CVVIII (2006), p. 495.

10 Richard Owen, *A History of British Fossil Mammals and Birds* (London, 1846), p. 554.

11 Peter Woodall, 'Kingfishers (Alcedinidae)', in *Handbook of the Birds of the World*, ed. del Hoyo, Elliott and Jordi Sargatal, vol. VI, p. 130.

12 Stig Walsh and Angela Milner, '*Halcyornis toliapicus* (Aves: Lower Eocene, England) Indicates Advanced Neuromorphology in Mesozoic Neornithes', *Journal of Systematic Paleontology*, IX (2011), p. 173.

13 Gerald Mayr, 'New Specimens of *Hassiavis laticauda* (Aves: Cypselomorphae) and *Quasisyndactylus longibrachis* (Aves: Alcediniformes) from the Middle Eocene of Messel, Germany', *Courier Forschungsinstitut Senckenberg*, CCLII (2004), pp. 23–8.

14 Caley, 'Fossil Birds', p. 38.

15 Woodall, 'Kingfishers (Alcedinidae)', p. 130.

16 Walter E. Boles, 'A Kingfisher (Halcyonidae) from the Miocene of Riversleigh, Northwestern Queensland, with Comments on the Evolution of Kingfishers in Australo-Papua', *Mem. Queensland Museum*, XLI (1997), pp. 229–34.

17 Woodall, 'Kingfishers (Alcedinidae)', p. 130.

18 Ibid., p. 130.

19 Alfred R. Wallace, 'A Monograph of the Alcedinidae, or Family of Kingfishers', *Nature*, III (1871), p. 467.

20 C. Hilary Fry and Kathie Fry, *Kingfishers, Bee-eaters and Rollers: A Handbook* (Princeton, NJ, 1992), p. 21.

21 Robert G. Moyle, 'A Molecular Phylogeny of Kingfishers (Alcedinidae) with Insights into Early Biogeographic History', *The Auk*, CXXIII (2006), p. 496.

22 Michael J. Andersen et al., 'A Phylogeny of Kingfishers Reveals an Indomalayan Origin and Elevated Rates of Diversification on Oceanic Islands', *Journal of Biogeography*, XLV (2017), pp. 268–81.

23 Wallace, 'A Monograph of the Alcedinidae', pp. 466–7.

24 Jenna McCullough, University of New Mexico, personal communication, 28 November 2017.

25 Moyle, 'A Molecular Phylogeny', p. 496.

26 Charles R. Darwin, *The Descent of Man* [1871], revd edn (New York, 1998), p. 396.

27 Michael J. Andersen et al., 'Rapid Diversification and a Secondary Sympatry in Australo-Pacific Kingfishers (Aves: Alcedinidae: *Todiramphus*)', *Royal Society Open Science* (2015), vol. II, p. 140375.

28 Andersen et al., 'A Phylogeny of Kingfishers', pp. 269–81.

2 KINGFISHERS UNMASKED

1 J.R.R. Tolkien, *The Hobbit* (London, 1937), p. 1.

2 Peter Woodall, 'Kingfishers (Alcedinidae)', in *Handbook of the Birds of the World*, ed. Josep del Hoyo, Andrew Elliott and Jordi Sargatal (Barcelona, 2001), vol. VI, p. 169.

3 Garry Marvin, *Wolf* (London, 2012), p. 21.

4 C. Hilary Fry and Kathie Fry, *Kingfishers, Bee-eaters and Rollers: A Handbook* (Princeton, NJ, 1992), p. 221.

5 Woodall, 'Kingfishers (Alcedinidae)', p. 158.

6 Ibid., p. 154.

7 Fry and Fry, *Kingfishers, Bee-eaters and Rollers*, p. 119.

8 Woodall, 'Kingfishers (Alcedinidae)', p. 169.

9 Ibid.

10 Ibid., p. 172.

11 Ibid.

12 Kathryn C. Gamble, 'Coraciiformes (Kingfishers, Motmots, Bee-eaters, Hoopoes, Hornbills)', in *Fowler's Zoo and Wild Animal Medicine*, ed. R. Eric Miller and Murray E. Fowler (Philadelphia, PA, 2014), vol. VIII, p. 226.

13 Heinz-Ulrich Reyer, 'Flexible Helper Structure as an Ecological Adaptation in the Pied Kingfisher (*Ceryle rudis rudis*)', *Behavioral Ecology and Sociobiology*, VI (1980), pp. 219–27.

14 Sarah Legge, *Kookaburra: King of the Bush* (Collingwood, VIC, 2004), p. 46.

15 Sarah Legge et al., 'Complex Sex Allocation in the Laughing Kookaburra', *Behavioral Ecology*, XII (2001), pp. 524–33.

16 Sarah Legge, 'Siblicide in the Cooperatively Breeding Laughing Kookaburra (*Dacelo novaeguineae*)', *Behavior Ecology and Sociobiology*, XLVIII (2000), pp. 293–302.

17 David Lack, *The Natural Regulation of Animal Numbers* (Oxford, 1954).

18 Boreal owls: Aaron Anderson et al., 'Siblicide and Cannibalism in Alaskan Boreal Owls', *Journal of Raptor Research*, XLIX (2015), pp. 498–500; barn owls: Sofi Hindmarsh, Simon Fraser University, personal communication, 7 March 2012; northern goshawks: W. Estes, S. Dewey and P. Kennedy, 'Siblicide at Northern Goshawk Nests: Does Food Play a Role?', *Wilson Bulletin*, CXI (1999), pp. 432–6; blue-footed boobies: Hugh Drummond, Cristina Rodrígues and Hubert Schwab, 'Do Mothers Regulate Facultative and Obligate Siblicide by Differentially Provisioning Eggs with Hormones?', *Journal of Avian Biology*, XXXIX (2008), pp. 139–43.

19 Rachel Warren Chadd and Marianne Taylor, *Birds: Myths, Lore and Legend* (London, 2016), p. 93.

20 'That Jungle Sound', http://soundandthefoley.com, accessed 30 May 2013.

21 'Ha Ha Ho Ho Ha Ha Ho Ho', *Sydney Morning Herald* (19 February 1983), www.newspapers.com.

22 Woodall, 'Kingfishers (Alcedinidae)', p. 154.

23 Marvin, *Wolf*, p. 25.

24 Woodall, 'Kingfishers (Alcedinidae)', p. 154.

25 Ibid.

26 *The History of Animals: Aristotle*, trans. D'Arcy Wentworth Thompson, (Gloucestershire, 1910), eBooks (Adelaide, 2015), vol. VIII/3.

27 Woodall, 'Kingfishers (Alcedinidae)', p. 154.

28 Ibid., p. 152.

29 Gamble, 'Coraciiformes', pp. 225–30.

30 Fry and Fry, *Kingfishers, Bee-eaters and Rollers*, p. 134.

31 Woodall, 'Kingfishers (Alcedinidae)', p. 166.

32 Ibid., p. 159.

33 Gary W. Kaiser, *The Inner Bird: Anatomy and Evolution* (Vancouver, 2007), p. 244.

34 Fry and Fry, *Kingfishers, Bee-eaters and Rollers*, p. 238.

35 Ibid., p. 220.

36 Ibid., p. 235.

37 Ibid., p. 220.

38 Beth Bahner, 'Extinct in the Wild: Partnering to Save the Guam Kingfisher' (22 June 2015), www.aquariumofpacific.org.

39 Joshua B. Smith et al., 'Brown Tree Snake (*Boiga irregularis*) Population Density and Carcass Locations Following Exposure to Acetaminophen', *Ecotoxicology*, xxv (2016), pp. 1556–62.

40 Bahner, 'Extinct in the Wild'; Scott Newland, Sedgwick County Zoo, personal communication, 4 December 2017.

3 CELESTIAL KINGFISHERS

1 *Ovid's Metamorphoses*, trans. Sir Samuel Garth et al. (London, 1717), p. 296.

2 Robert Graves, *The Greek Myths* (London, 1955), pp. 163–5.

3 *Compete Works of Aristotle: The Revised Oxford Translation*, ed. Jonathan Barnes (Princeton, NJ, 1984), vol. I.

4 Rozenn Bailleul-LeSuer, 'Between Heaven and Earth: Birds in Ancient Egypt', *Oriental Institute of the University of Chicago Publication*, xxxv (2013), p. 57.

5 Cottie Burland, Irene Nicholson and Harold Osborne, *Mythology of the Americas* (London, 1970), pp. 69–70.

6 Peter Woodall, 'Kingfishers (Alcedinidae)', in *Handbook of the Birds of the World*, ed. Josep del Hoyo, Andrew Elliott and Jordi Sargatal (Barcelona, 2001), vol. VI, p. 181.

7 Jan M. Mike, *The Sun and the Kookaburra: An Aboriginal Folktale from Australia* (New York, 1997), pp. 1–16.

8 Amy Friedman and Meredith Johnson, *Kookaburra's Laughter: An Australian Legend* (25 June 2006), https://uexpress.com/tell-me-a-story/2006/6/25/kookaburras-laughter-an-australian-legend.

9 J. A. Farrer, 'Animal Lore in Sylvanus Urban', *Gentleman's Magazine*, CCLXI (1886), p. 593.

10 Peter Tate, *Flights of Fancy: Birds in Myth, Legend and Superstition* (New York, 2007), p. 68.

11 Ibid.

12 Kingdom, *Johnny Kingdom's West Country Tales*, p. 177.

13 Ibid.

14 'Migratory Birds of the Great Lakes: Belted Kingfisher', http://seagrant.wisc.edu, accessed 13 October 2016.

15 'Bird Stories, Grey-winged Trumpeter (*Psophia crepitans*)', *Planet of Birds: Source to All Birds on the Planet* (12 May 2013), http://planetofbirds.com.

16 Dorothy Tanner, *Legends of the Red Man's Forest* (Chicago, IL, 1895), p. 59.

17 Farrer, 'Animal Lore in Sylvanus Urban', p. 597.

18 'The Fox and the Kingfisher: A Jicarilla Apache Legend', www.firstpeople.us, accessed 16 April 2017.

19 Ariel Cohen, 'Rattles', https://haidatlingit.wordpress.com, accessed 10 September 2017.

20 Philip Lutgendorf, *Hanuman's Tale: The Messages of a Divine Monkey* (Oxford, 2007), p. 160.

21 Woodall, 'Kingfishers (Alcedinidae)', p. 180.

22 Anne Salmond, *The Trial of the Cannibal Dog: The Remarkable Story of Captain Cook's Encounters in the South Seas* (New Haven, CT, 2003), p. 205.

23 Ibid., p. 208.

24 George Turner, *Samoa, A Hundred Years Ago and Long Before: Together with Notes on the Cults* (London, 1884), p. 48.

25 Kelly Keane, 'Ngā manu – birds, 5: Sayings, metaphors and stories' (24 September 2007), https://teara.govt.nz.

1 Paul W. Kroll, 'The Image of the Halcyon Kingfisher in Medieval Chinese Poetry', *Journal of the American Oriental Society*, CIV (1984), p. 238.
2 April Liu, Mellon Postdoctoral Curatorial Fellow, University of British Columbia Museum of Anthropology, personal communication, 9 August 2017.
3 Kroll, 'The Image of the Halcyon Kingfisher', p. 241.
4 David Quammem, *The Song of the Dodo: Island Biogeography in an Age of Extinction* (New York, 1996), p. 316.
5 Beverly Jackson, *Kingfisher Blue: Treasures of an Ancient Art* (Berkeley, CA, 2001), p. 84.
6 Ibid., p. 130.
7 Ibid., p. 97.
8 Ibid., p. 49.
9 Ibid., p. 52.
10 Ibid., p. 49.
11 Ibid., p. 193.
12 Geoffrey E. Hill and Kevin J. McGraw, *Bird Coloration,* vol. I: *Mechanism and Measurements* (Cambridge, MA, 2006), pp. 328–33.
13 Kroll, 'The Image of the Halcyon Kingfisher', p. 238. Translation author's own.
14 Jackson, *Kingfisher Blue*, p. 22.
15 Edward Schafer, quoted in Kroll, 'The Image of the Halcyon Kingfisher in Medieval Chinese Poetry', p. 238.
16 Osbert Sitwell, *Escape with Me! An Oriental Sketch-book* (London, 1949), pp. 141–2.
17 Charles Higham, *The Civilization of Angkor* (London, 2001), pp. xiii–xiv.
18 John Tully, *A Short History of Cambodia: from Empire to Survival* (Sydney, 2005), p. 17; Bernard P. Groslier, 'La Cité Hydraulique Angkorienne: Exploitation ou Surexploitation du Sol?', *Bulletin de l'Ecole française d'Extrême-Orient*, LXVI (1976), pp. 161–202;

Roland Fletcher et al., 'A Comprehensive Archaeological
Map of the World's Largest Preindustrial Settlement Complex
at Angkor, Cambodia', *Proceedings of the National Academy of
Sciences of the United States of America*, CIV (2007), pp. 14277–82.

19 Sitwell, *Escape with Me!*, pp. 140–41.

20 Barbara A. West, *Encyclopedia of the Peoples of Asia and Oceania*
(New York, 2009), p. 397.

21 Adrien von Ferscht, 'Treasured Kingfisher Feathers Give Chinese
Export Silver the Blues', www.worthpoint.com (6 September 2013).

22 Tully, *A Short History of Cambodia*, pp. 52–4.

23 Ibid., p. 53.

24 Ibid., p. 17.

5 INFLUENTIAL KINGFISHERS

1 Clifford B. Frith, *Charles Darwin's Life with Birds: His Complete
Ornithology* (New York, 2016), p. 25.

2 Julia Voss, *Darwin's Pictures: Views on Evolutionary Theory,
1837–1874* [2007], trans. Lori Lantz (New Haven, CT, 2010),
p. 49.

3 Ibid.

4 Frank D. Steinheimer, 'Charles Darwin's Bird Collection
and Ornithological Knowledge During the Voyage of HMS
Beagle, 1831–1836', *Journal of Ornithology*, CXLV (2004),
pp. 300–320.

5 David Quammen, *The Reluctant Mr Darwin: An Intimate Portrait
of Charles Darwin and the Making of His Theory of Evolution*
(New York, 2006), p. 34.

6 Ibid., p. 35.

7 Charles Darwin, *The Correspondence of Charles Darwin*, vol. XV: *1867*
(Cambridge, 2006), p. 99.

8 Ibid., p. 183.

9 Charles R. Darwin, *The Expression of the Emotions in Man and
Animals* [1904], ed. Francis Darwin, p. 50; in Frith, *Charles Darwin's
Life with Birds*, p. 200.

10 Ernst Mayr, 'Darwin's Influence on Modern Thought', *Scientific American* (July 2000), pp. 79–83, https://scientificamerican.com, accessed 7 July 2017.

11 Carl G. Jung, *Memories, Dreams, Reflections* (New York, 1989), p. 183.

12 James Thurber, *Further Fables of our Times* (London, 1956), p. 138.

13 *Aesop's Fables*, illus. by Maud U. Clarke (Bristol, 2013), p. 102.

14 Karen Edwards, 'Milton's Reformed Animals: An Early Modern Bestiary H–K', *Milton Quarterly*, XLI/2 (2007), p. 79.

15 Walt Whitman, 'Halcyon Days', The Walt Whitman Archive: Periodicals, http://whitmanarchive.org, accessed 29 July 2017.

16 Eugene H. Peterson, *As Kingfishers Catch Fire: A Conversation on the Ways of God Formed by the Words of God* (New York, 2017); Alex Preston and Neil Grower, *As Kingfishers Catch Fire: Books and Birds* (London, 2017).

17 *Ovid's Metamorphoses*: *The Arthur Golding Translation, 1567*, ed. John Frederick Nims (Philadelphia, PA, 2000), p. XVIII.

18 Charles Olson, 'Projective Verse', https://poetryfoundation.org, accessed 13 October 2009.

19 Peter Tate, *Flights of Fancy: Birds in Myth, Legend and Superstition* (New York, 2007), pp. 70–71.

20 Ernest Ingersoll, *Birds in Legends, Fable and Folklore* (New York, 1923), p. 239.

21 Edwin Radford and Mona Augusta Radford, *The Encyclopedia of Superstitions* [1949], revd Christina Hole (London, 2002), p. 209.

22 Tate, *Flights of Fancy*, p.146.

23 Ingersoll, *Birds in Legends*, p. 23.

24 Giraldus Cambrensis, '*Topographia Hibernica*' [1188], trans. Thomas Forester, in *Topography of Ireland* (Cambridge, ON, 2000), p. 38.

25 John A. Wilson, *The Culture of Ancient Egypt* (Chicago, IL, 1951), p. 219.

26 'Pre-Raphaelites: The Bad Boys Who Painted in Plein Air' (27 November 2012), www.worldpress.com.

27 Van Gogh Museum, *Kingfisher by the Waterside*, www.vangoghmuseum.nl/en, accessed 12 May 2018.

28 Ella Hendriks and Louis van Tilborgh, *The Vincent van Gogh Paintings*, vol. II: *Antwerp and Paris, 1885–1888* (London, 2011), p. 448.

29 Van Gogh Museum, *The Kingfisher*, www.vangoghmuseum.nl, accessed 12 May 2018.

30 J. O. Halliwell, ed., *The Metrical History of Tom Thumb the Little* (London, 1860), p. 7; *Playhour Annual*, 143 (London, 1957).

6 ICONIC KINGFISHERS

1 Penny Reed, Visitor Marketing Coordinator at the Wildfowl & Wetlands Trust (WWT), personal communication, 9 December 2016.

2 'Legacy – History of the EBFC, 1970's to 1990's', www.eastbengalfootballclub.com, accessed 30 July 2017.

3 Bill Burns, 'Halcyon-class Ships', www.halcyon-class.co.uk, accessed 29 July 2017.

4 Mark Barber, 'Ugly Ducklings: The Vought OS2U Kingfisher', http://warthunder.com/en, accessed 30 July 2017.

5 Norman MacCaig, *The Poems of Norman MacCaig* (Ann Arbor, MI, 2005), p. 327.

7 MASTERS OF TWO MEDIUMS

1 Tom McKeag, 'How One Engineer's Birdwatching Made Japan's Bullet Train Better', www.greenbiz.com (12 October 2012).

2 'JFS Biomimicry Interview Series: No. 6: Shinkansen Technology Learned from an Owl? The Story of Eiji Nakatsu', *Japan for Sustainability* (March 2005), http://japanfs.org.

3 Ibid.

Select Bibliography

Andersen, Michael J., et al., 'A Phylogeny of Kingfisher
    Reveals an Indomalayan Origin and Elevated Rates of
    Diversification on Oceanic Islands', *Journal of Biogeography*,
    XLV (2018)

Bate, Jonathan, 'Shakespeare's Ovid', in *Ovid's Metamorphoses:
    The Arthur Golding Translation (1567)*, ed. John Frederick Nims
    (Philadelphia, PA, 2000)

Chadd, Rachel Warren, and Marianne Taylor, *Birds: Myth, Lore and
    Legend* (London, 2016)

Darwin, Charles R., *The Descent of Man* [1871], revd edn
    (New York, 1998)

Firth, Clifford B., *Charles Darwin's Life with Birds: His Complete
    Ornithology* (New York, 2016)

Fry, C. Hilary, and Kathie Fry, *Kingfishers, Bee-eaters and Rollers:
    A Handbook* (Princeton, NJ, 1992)

Jackson, Beverly, *Kingfisher Blue: Treasures of an Ancient Art*
    (Berkeley, CA, 2001)

Jaffe, Mark, *And No Birds Sing: A Story of an Ecological Disaster in a
    Tropical Paradise* (New York, 1994)

Mayr, Gerald, 'New Specimens of *Hassiavis laticauda* (Aves:
    Cypselomorphae) and *Quasisyndactylus longibrachis* (Aves:
    Alcediniformes) from the Middle Eocene of Messel, Germany',
    Courier Forschungsinstitut Senckenberg, CCLII (2004), pp. 23–8

Quammen, David, *The Reluctant Mr Darwin: An Intimate Portrait
    of Charles Darwin and the Making of his Theory of Evolution*
    (New York, 2006)

—, *The Song of the Dodo: Island Biogeography in an Age of Extinctions*
(New York, 1996)

Schwab, Ivan R., *Evolution's Witness: How Eyes Evolved* (Oxford, 2012)

Sharpe, Richard Bowdler, *A Monograph of the Alcedinidae; or, Family
of Kingfishers* (London, 1871)

Tate, Peter, *Flights of Fancy: Birds in Myth, Legend and Superstition*
(London, 2007)

Tully, John, *A Short History of Cambodia: From Empire to Survival*
(Crows Nest, NSW, 2005)

Woodall, Peter, 'Kingfishers (Alcedinidae)', in *Handbook of the Birds
of the World*, ed. Josep del Hoyo, Andrew Elliott and Jordi Sargatal
(Barcelona, 2001), vol. VI, pp. 130–249

ONLINE VIDEOS

Bahner, Beth, *Extinct in the Wild: Partnering to Save the Guam Kingfisher*,
www.aquariumofpacific.org, 22 June 2015

McCue, Michael, and USDA APHIS, *Battling the Brown Tree Snake Aerial
Bait Drops on Guam*, www.youtube.com, 26 August 2016

Acknowledgements

Finishing a book commonly results in your work/life balance going the way of the dodo. Having friends and family who understand that you are in this 'other reality' as the deadline approaches is essential. Their willingness to accept your neglect, your non-participation in life, yet give their full support in the measly little time chunks you reluctantly devote to being normal, is key. My family and friends have been exceptional.

Many thanks to my chief sounding boards Roger Hanna, Ray Hryciuk and Sheila Byers, and to the UBC work-learn students for being enthusiastic about everything; and especially to Christopher M. Stinson for enduring my absentmindedness of late. My colleagues at the University of British Columbia Museum of Anthropology and the Beaty Biodiversity Museum are, as with all my endeavours, extremely supportive and inspiring.

Special thanks are due to the curatorial staff of the National Museum of Natural History, Washington, DC; the Muséum National d'Histoire Naturelle, Paris; and the Natural History Museum at Tring. Jenna McCullough of the University of New Mexico Andersen Lab, Albuquerque kindly kept me informed about upcoming changes to kingfisher systematics. It is incredible, and extremely appreciated, that Jenna somehow found the time while writing her PhD thesis to create a custom version of the kingfisher cladogram for inclusion in this book. Markus Lilje of Rockjumper Birding Tours deserves a special mention for having supplied Jenna with the necessary images, plus contributing so many photographs to this project.

A big thank you to series editor Jonathan Burt for responding so positively that adding a kingfisher book to his wonderful Animal series should happen. This project began due to a serendipitous encounter with

Daniel Heath Justice (*Badger*) cemented by Rachel Poliquin (*Beaver*), both of whom affirmed that contributing to this series was an adventure worth having. Thank you to Michael Leaman, publisher, for answering all my questions and being indispensable throughout this journey. Another round of thanks to Jonathan and Michael for finding the best elements in my first draft and inviting me to expand upon them. Working with picture editor Harry Gilonis on the images, and harder still with editor Phoebe Colley on the proofs, has been a great honour and pleasure. To the rest of the staff at Reaktion Books, who I have never spoken to but are tolling in the background, I thank you all from the bottom of my heart.

Above all, I thank my tireless mother, Eve Szabo. Though she despaired that her ten-year-old dyslexic daughter would ever learn to read, she never gave up. Your indomitable spirit lives on in this book. Thank you for making me learn the impossible, arousing my intellectual curiosity about nature – and, most of all, because of your love of kingfishers.

Photo Acknowledgements

The author and publishers wish to express their thanks to the following sources of illustrative material and/or permission to reproduce it. Some locations are also supplied here for reasons of brevity.

Photo © Ashmolean Museum, Oxford/Mary Evans Picture Library: p. 16; photos the author: pp. 12, 33, 54, 59; reproduced courtesy of the City of Blacktown, New South Wales: p. 153 (top); from Neltje Blanchan, *Bird Neighbors: An Introductory Acquaintance with One Hundred and Fifty Birds Commonly Found in the Gardens, Meadows, and Woods About Our Homes* (Garden City, NY, 1916): p. 93; photo blickwinkel/Alamy Stock Photo: p. 10; from William Brigham, 'Additional Notes on Hawaiian Feather Work', supplement to *Memoirs of the Bernice Pauahi Bishop Museum of Polynesian Ethnology and Natural History*, vol. VII, no. 1 (Honolulu, HI, 1918): p. 102; photos Peter Candido: pp. 66, 127; from the *Catalogue of Birds in the British Museum*, vol. XVII (London, 1892): p. 126; photo Cornell University Library: p. 56; from George Edwards, *Sammlung verschneider ausländischer und seltener Vogel* (Nuremberg, 1749–76): p. 17; Egyptian Museum of Antiquities, Cairo: p. 141; Heritage Image Partnership Ltd/Alamy Stock Photo: p. 128; Houghton Library, Harvard University (John James Audubon Letters and Drawings, 1805–92, MS Am 21 [50]: p. 38; J. Paul Getty Museum, Malibu (Open Access): p. 90; photo James Leyland/Alamy Stock Photo: p. 6; photo Library of Congress, Washington, DC: 158 (Prints and Photographs Division – Office of War Information – Overseas Picture Division – Washington Division); photos Markus Lilje, Rockjumper Bird Tours: pp. 20, 37, 44, 47, 112; Los Angeles County Museum of Art (Open Access): p. 148; photo Quinn A. McCallum: p. 25;

Jenna M. McCullough (Andersen Lab, University of New Mexico), using bird images supplied by Markus Lilje, Rockjumper Bird Tours: p. 32; reproduced courtesy of the City of Maroondah, Victoria: p. 154; Metropolitan Museum of Art: pp. 111, 131; photos Metropolitan Museum of Art (Open Access): pp. 87, 111, 131, 156; reproduced by kind permission of the artist (Charlotte Montanaro): pp. 69, 77; Museum of Anthropology at the University of British Columbia, Vancouver: pp. 96 (photo Rebecca Pasch), 100 (photo Jessica Bushey), 101 (photo Derek Tan), 103 (photo Jessica Bushey), 106 (photo Kyla Bailey) – all images © UBC Museum of Anthropology; Museums Victoria Collections, Melbourne: p. 60; National Gallery of Art, Washington, DC: pp. 138, 144, 146 (Open Access): National Museum of Wales, Cardiff: p. 86; Natural History Museum, London (photo Mary Evans Picture Library/Natural History Museum): p. 97; The Natural History Museum at Tring (Natural History Museum, London): p. 122; Neuschwanstein Castle, Bavaria: p. 140; from *Novitates Zoologicae: A Journal of Zoology,* vol. IX (1902): p. 143; photo Vicki Nunn: p. 72; Palace Museum, Beijing: p. 110; photo A. Parrot: p. 141; from *Picture Alphabet of Birds* (London and Edinburgh, 1874): p. 150; private collection: p. 11; from Chester Albert Reed, *American Ornithology for the Home and School* (Worcester, MA, 1901) – photo Smithsonian Libraries: p. 13; from Ludwig Richter, *Neue Fabeln . . .* (Leipzig, 1846): p. 130 (photo Library of Congress Prints and Photographs Division, Washington, DC); from Hermann Schlegel, *De vogels van Nederlandsch Indië beschreven en afgebeeld door H. Schlegel*, vol. II (Haarlem, 1869): p. 57; from R. Bowdler Sharpe, *Wonders of the Bird World* (New York, 1921): p. 56; photo Smithsonian Libraries: p. 13; Smithsonian Museum of Natural History, Washington, DC: pp. 54 [Division of Birds, B28122, 1 nest, *Chloroceryle americana*, U.S., Texas, Bexar, San Antonio, Medura River, 28 March 1896], 59 [Division of Birds, B47649, eggs, *Ceryle alcyon*, North Freedom, Wisconsin, 24 May 1903]; photos Special Collections of the University of Amsterdam: pp. 57, 94; from 'The Story of Tom Thumb' in *Playhour* (1957): p. 151 (photo Mary Evans Picture Library/*Playhour*); Tallinn Museum of Orders: p. 9; Tate Britain, London: p. 147 foot); John Thompson, *Illustrations of China and its People: A Series of Two Hundred Photographs, with Letterpress Descriptive of the Places and People Represented*, vol. IV, 'Illustrations of China' (London, 1874): p. 105; photo by Sven Tränkner, reproduced by permission of Gerald May, Forschungsinstitut Senckenberg, Frankfurt am Main: p. 27; Van Gogh Museum, Nederlands: p. 147 (top); photo Sias van Schalkwyk: p. 39; from Alfred Russel Wallace, *The Geographical Distribution of Animals, with a Study of the Relations of Living and Extinct Faunas as Elucidating the Past Changes of the Earth's Surface*, vol. I (London, 1876): p. 28; Walters Art Museum, Baltimore: pp. 76, 104, 119; whereabouts unknown: p. 79; photo Yale University Library, New Haven (Beinecke Rare Books and Manuscript Library): p. 105.

Andy Morffew, the copyright holder of the images on pp. 8, 53, 164 and 165 (foot), dw_ross, the copyright holder of the image on p. 80, jasonbkk, the copyright holder of the image on p. 45, and tjabeljan, the copyright holder of the image on p. 155, have published them online under conditions imposed by a Creative Commons Attribution 2.0 Generic license; Bernard DUPONT, the copyright holder of the images on pp. 34 and 40, Dennis Jarvis, the copyright holder of the image on p. 118, Jim Bendon, the copyright holder of the image on p. 46, and Markus Lilje, the copyright holder of the image on p. 42, have published them online under conditions imposed by a Creative Commons Attribution 2.0 Generic license; I·lustraciència/ACCC, the copyright holder of the image on p. 77 (reproduced by kind permission of the artist [Charlotte Montanaro], and JJ Harrison, the copyright holder of the image on p. 48, have published them online under conditions imposed by a Creative Commons Attribution-Share Alike 3.0 Unported license; AjitK332, the copyright holder of the image on p. 43, Anup Deodha, the copyright holder of the image on p. 86, Artemy Voikhansky, the copyright holder of the image on p. 165 (top), Borodun, the copyright holder of the image on p. 9, photo CoinInvest GmbH, the copyright holder of the image on p. 160, Laitche, the copyright holder of the image on p. 114, Manoj Karingamadathil, the copyright holder of the image on p. 82, Marcin Konsek/Wikimedia Commons/CC BY-SA 4.0, the copyright holder of the image on p. 74, Museums Victoria, the copyright holder of the image on p. 60, Prateik Kulkarni, the copyright holder of the image on p. 49, Richard Stephen

Haynes the copyright holder of the image on p. 159, Satdeep Gill, the copyright holder of the image on p. 102, Charles J. Sharp (Sharp-photography), the copyright holder of the images on pp. 21 and 70–71, and TARUNJYOTI TEWARI, the copyright holder of the image on p. 109, have published them online under conditions imposed by a Creative Commons Attribution-Share Alike 4.0 International license; Bernard Gagnon, the copyright holder of the image on p. 65, has published it online under conditions imposed by a Creative Commons Attribution-Share Alike 4.0 International, 3.0 Unported, 2.5 Generic, 2.0 Generic and 1.0 Generic license.

Readers are free to share – to copy, distribute and transmit these images alone; to remix – to adapt these images alone – under the following conditions: attribution – readers must attribute either image in the manner specified by the author or licensor (but not in any way that suggests that these parties endorse them or their use of the work), and share alike: if readers alter, transform, or build upon this image, they may distribute the resulting work only under the same or similar license to this one.

Wellcome Images, the copyright holder of the image on p. 15, have licensed it under a Creative Commons Attribution 4.0 International license. Readers are free to share – to copy and redistribute this work/these works – or to adapt – to remix, transform and build upon this work/these works for any purpose, even commercially, under the following conditions: they must attribute the work(s) in the manner specified by the author or licensor (but not in any way that suggests that they endorse you or your use of the work[s]) and if they alter, transform, or build upon the work, they may distribute the resulting work(s) only under the same or similar licenses to those listed above). They may not apply legal terms or technological measures that legally restrict others from doing anything the license permits.

Prathyush Thomas, copyright holder of the work reproduced on p. 115, hereby publishes it under the following licenses: Permission is granted

Index